147 Practical Tips for Teaching Diversity

By William Timpson
Raymond Yang
Evelinn Borrayo
and Silvia Sara Canetto

Atwood Publishing
Madison, WI

147 Practical Tips for Teaching Diversity
By William Timpson, Raymond Yang, Evelinn Borrayo, and Silvia Sara Canetto
© 2005 Atwood Publishing, Madison, WI
www.atwoodpublishing.com

Cover design by Tamara Dever, TLC Graphics, www.tlcgraphics.com

Library of Congress Cataloging-in-Publication Data

147 practical tips for teaching diversity / by William Timpson ... [et al.].
    p. cm.
  Includes bibliographical references.
  ISBN 1-891859-50-1 (pbk.)
  1. Multicultural education—United States. 2. College teaching—United States. I.
Title: One hundred forty-seven practical tips for teaching diversity. II. Timpson,
William M.

  LC1099.3.A16 2005
  370.117—dc22

                              2005003007

Acknowledgments

Our thanks go again to our sixteen colleagues who contributed to our companion volume, *Teaching Diversity,* also from Atwood Publishing; to Linda Babler, our editor, whose *147 Practical Tips* series provided the framework we needed to get to these concise and practical sets of ideas and recommendations; and to Bob Magnan, who provided a final editorial polish.

Dedication

To all our students —
your learning has been our reference,
your growth has been our challenge,
your openness has been our joy,
and your very presence has been a gift.

Table of Contents

Develop Your Instructional Skills 55

Communicate and Collaborate 61

Challenge Ideas, Attitudes, and Beliefs 66

Introduction

Twenty of us, faculty and staff, spent three years discussing the classroom questions associated with teaching about human diversity: How do we improve our own teaching? How do we reach students who were resistant or angry? Where do we turn for help from our own university? How do we overcome our isolation as teachers, share ideas, and explore new possibilities? How do we face our own prejudices? Where do we put diversity content in courses already bulging with content?

The book that resulted, *Teaching Diversity: Challenges and Complexities, Identities and Integrity* (2003) sparked some wonderfully complex discussions and debates as we reflected on our own classes and attempted to find what was useful to others. We shared readings and circulated drafts of our writing as we struggled to understand the meaning of "best practice."

No one was paid for any of this. We were never appointed as a formal committee or task force. We were excited to be contributing something new to the scholarship of teaching on a subject that was inherently interesting, challenging, and difficult. As every campus struggles to live up to its promises about increasing diversity, holding the usual workshops and hosting various invited speakers, we had found a mechanism for getting deep and protracted contributions from instructors on the front lines of diversity work.

In *147 Practical Tips for Teaching Diversity*, we present concrete ideas for addressing the various issues that surface when teaching about human diversity. We cite sources, particularly *Teaching Diversity*, so that you can easily read more about any one particular idea.

Raymond Yang suggests the following guide for using these tips:

BEFORE THE COURSE BEGINS:

- Embrace a pedagogy of human diversity

EARLY IN THE COURSE:

- Develop rapport, community, and emotional maturity
- Create safe, open, inclusive, and supportive classrooms

THROUGHOUT THE COURSE:

- Expand and deepen student thinking
- Support student-centered learning
- Face conflicts with intelligence, sensitivity, and creativity
- Unlearn stereotyping and prejudice
- Develop your instructional skills
- Communicate and collaborate
- Challenge ideas, attitudes, and beliefs
- Support positive change
- Support personal and professional development
- Support diversity by globalizing the curriculum

AFTER THE END OF THE COURSE:

- Rethink curriculum and expectations
- Contribute to the scholarship of teaching diversity
- Deepen your institution's commitment to diversity

Enjoy!

Embrace a Pedagogy of Human Diversity

With all the pressures on instructors to be disciplinary experts, scholars, and researchers, there is precious little time and far too few resources dedicated to instructional improvement, innovation, and effectiveness. In this section, we offer grounded ideas for rethinking instruction through a focus on diversity content, an area fraught with challenges and complexities.

1. See differences as constructed and real.

There is a certain sophistication of thought required for addressing instructional issues related to diversity. Simplistic generalizations risk creating new stereotypes, assumptions that *all* members of this or that group believe or behave in a certain manner.

When first discussing issues of diversity, you can brainstorm about some common stereotypes about women and men, college students and professors, and people from rural, urban, and suburban areas. Check with your students about the accuracy of each stereotype for them, using a scale of one (low) to five (high).

As Silvia Sara Canetto, William Timpson, Evelinn Borrayo, and Raymond Yang (2003, 276) state, a definition of diversity "acknowledges how categories of 'difference' (e.g., ethnic classifications) are historically and culturally produced constructs, yet still affirms that these categories of differences have enormous real and practical consequences for the lives of individuals at a particular time and place."

2. Honor expertise on diversity.

Assess your own knowledge to teach the diversity components of your classes. Identify areas of strength and needed growth. Make a plan for reading. List other experiences that would be useful. Make appointments to consult with colleagues who also have diversity content in their courses.

Emphasizing the expertise needed to teach effectively about diversity can avoid marginalizing this content and ensure that students get the kind of skilled facilitation they need to navigate complex, sensitive material.

3. Be inclusive and note intersections.

Complexities abound as variables such as ethnicity, age, socioeconomic class, gender, background, preparation, motivation, resources, and instructor skills and beliefs interact to impact learning.

Have your students list all the various categories that they themselves represent. Ask which variables intersect to impact their learning, e.g., single working mothers, unemployed older men, creative and active individuals who struggle with straight lecture courses. Discuss how your course could be both *inclusive* of multiple categories and *attentive* to the attendant complexities.

Canetto, Timpson, Borrayo, and Yang (2003, 276) summarize these effects in this way:

> [A] pedagogy of human diversity ... is both inclusive of multiple categories of social classification as well as attentive to the complexities of human experience when different categories intersect (e.g., gender and ethnicity).

4. Study diversity.

As instructors, we can work toward understanding the contributions of diverse individuals to our own disciplines. We can profit from various readings — from reports and biographies, to the mass of primary sources yet to be discovered. Make a plan to research areas of diversity for your own classes.

5. Examine policies and court decisions.

Beyond the rhetoric of acceptance and tolerance are the hard facts of life for many diverse peoples within a dominant culture. A focus on

laws, policies, and primary sources can help remove the haze of denial that often shrouds brutal reality.

Identify legal and public policy issues in your own discipline. Ask students how these are impacted by questions of culture and by questions of power.

6. Understand similarities.

A preoccupation with differences can blind us to what we have in common. People can make huge leaps in overcoming prejudices and find acceptance when they realize that there are almost always greater differences *within* any group — height, weight, age, background, interests, abilities, motivations, etc. — than ever exist *between* groups that may differ along ethnic lines, gender, religious background, sexual orientation, etc.

Have the students identify their similarities. Next explore the range of variation within the men and within the women. Invariably, there will be many more differences within any particular group than between and among groups. Repeat this with other categories.

Expand and Deepen Student Thinking

A pedagogy of human diversity demands that we move past simple and dichotomous thinking to embrace more of what psychologist William Perry (1999) defines as the ability to handle complexity and ambiguity, to understand the perspectives of others, and to seek coherence in reasoning.

7. Welcome contradictions and get students to think on the edge of their comfort zones.

A book of tips on teaching diversity might be misleading if instructors believe that handling the inherent mix of intellectual and emotional factors is a simple matter. In fact, one of our most important tips is to expect a challenge. Tell students that you will be deliberately provocative at times, that you will "play the devil's advocate" in order to spark deeper analyses.

Nina Roberts (2003, 233) contends that instructors should both encourage and challenge students, getting them to express themselves fully, and then validate (acknowledge, accept) their feelings and beliefs. Instructors should spark open, even heated, discussions — "I ... feel the need to respond in a way that broadens their thinking and puts them on the edge of their comfort zone" — but require respectful dialogue from everyone.

8. Connect thinking and personal experience to research.

Identify areas where you can distinguish between what has support in the research literature, what is still under debate, and what your own beliefs may be. Have students do the same on an issue of their choosing.

Many instructors struggle with the balance between supporting diverse opinions in an open, accepting, and inclusive classroom environment and drawing on research to outline more studied and objective attention to problems and solutions. Mona Schatz (2003, 126) states: "I try to blend research-based material with prevailing ideas, thereby sharpening the experience for students and giving them an 'edge' in critical and creative thinking and doing."

Many classes get stuck on a level where everybody's entitled to his or her own opinion without the skills needed to push further into the realm of evidence or support. Rosemary Kreston (2003, 183) tells of her experiences in teaching a course on disabilities and diversity.

> When I first started teaching this course alone, class evaluations indicated that some students felt I was too judgmental, too opinionated, or too biased in presenting information. As a result, I began to differentiate between opinion and fact or research more deliberately. I added qualifying words to statements so that data would not be interpreted as absolute. Separating my experience from researched knowledge has taken a great deal of self- examination so that I can offer useful insight without appearing biased.

9. Analyze terms, concepts, and the deeper meaning of language.

Choice of words and the use of language have much to do with how we think. Identify an important concept in your discipline that has implications for diversity, such as recruitment and retention of students. Explore the range of institutional responses that might be possible and the implications of putting a particular change into practice. Focus on the precision with which you think about that concept.

Stopping to reflect, to analyze, and to assess terms can begin to remove fundamental barriers to thinking. Silvia Sara Canetto, William Timpson, Evelinn Borrayo, and Raymond Yang (2003, 277) affirm that analyzing terms and concepts "can lead to more precise, sophisticated, and more socially sensitive thinking. It can also generate new insights about what teaching about human diversity means and what is required of teachers and students along the way."

When debates swirl around the language that people use to refer to this or that group, some will see a dampening effect on classroom discourse, an excessive sensitivity, and a concern for political correctness. However, language matters. Val Middleton (2003, 108) explains:

> I purposely try to use examples, nouns, and pronouns that are inclusive and diverse. ... I often use 'dominant culture status' as a term because the issues of diversity are so much broader than skin color. It is also important for me to let them know that it is not 'me against them,' because I too, at times, have dominant-culture status as an educated, middle-class, able-bodied person.

10. Introduce new ways of thinking.

Progress often hinges on overturning old and problematic concepts and finding new, creative ways forward. Rethink some of the concepts you or your texts have been using and explore the possibilities of new language. For example, Roe Bubar and Irene Vernon (2003, 162) have drawn on their legal training for materials, approaches, and language as they confront years of discriminatory policies and practices toward Native Americans.

> First, we begin teaching by helping students understand the 'study of law.' Law is a difficult subject matter, with an 'elitist' jargon that typically requires students to purchase a separate legal dictionary to complete reading assignments. It involves a new way of thinking. ... We expect students to learn this new legal language, to brief legal cases, and to participate in moot court arguments.

11. Pause for reflection.

Students are often overwhelmed with the amount of information that comes at them in class. Discussions can also be problematic when opinions range widely and students are unsure what to focus on and put into their notes. Find ways of pausing in class for you and your students to reflect. Use a brief, in-class free-write, or try counting silently to yourself to provide a little more "wait time" to help some students come up with thoughtful responses to complex questions. Pause and review periodically to help underscore key points and reinforce a conceptual framework that helps to keep everything connected.

Mona Schatz (2003, 130) offers the following suggestion:

You can have the group take short breaks in order to summarize the learning that has occurred and identify the range of expressions that have surfaced. In the process of recapping, you can seize the opportunity to acknowledge any emotional content that was expressed.

Students are often consumed by taking notes, especially when a lecture is fast-paced, when there is a flood of PowerPoint information to copy, or when the instructor is determined to cover everything promised. In classes like this, students have little if any opportunity to reflect, to integrate previous material, or apply what's being presented. To encourage more thoughtful consideration, Raymond Yang (2003, 86) periodically relieves his students of the burden of taking notes: "I instruct my students not to take notes and reassure them that the material covered will not show up on the next test. These steps establish an ambiance of safety in which students become more willing to express opinions and disclose ... experiences." At some point, he will then signal that his students can resume taking notes.

Finally, you too should pause to reflect. When problems surface in class, when things don't go as well as planned, when your confidence as an instructor is shaken, take some time to yourself to reflect honestly on events and your own reactions. You might find the spark for a new and creative insight during the time that these conflicts incubate in your mind and heart.

12. Celebrate initiative.

Personal initiative, in terms of the framework established by Perry (1981;1999), develops as students progress from thinking in terms of dichotomies (right/wrong, yes/no), a stage in which agency (authority) is external (in the teacher and the texts), toward accepting different opinions and becoming more able to handle complexity and ambiguity, a stage in which agency is internal (within themselves) (Timpson, Canetto, Borrayo, and Yang, 2003, 17).

Personal initiative is essential for learning to really take hold and evolve, especially when the content may be sensitive, complex, and emotional. Share instances from your own life, such as when your initiative helped you break down some of your own prejudices.

13. Emphasize critical thinking.

At its core, a college or university education has always meant questioning even the most cherished of traditional beliefs, searching for better explanations, and being open to the dictates of evidence, logic, and argument.

Encourage your students to think critically. Have them write down a particular point they want to make and then list the support that exists for that point. Have students pair off and each partner critique the other's arguments. Then, ask for students to volunteer to have all of their classmates critique their arguments. Affirm the value of this kind of critical analysis for any issue of importance.

Learning will increase as students move beyond simplistic, dichotomous expectations about right/wrong answers and become more able to accept varied opinions and multiple perspectives. Learning will deepen when students can go beyond merely accepting differences and ask about the coherent logic of the underlying reasoning.

Consider how Roe Bubar and Irene Vernon (2003, 161) emphasize critical thinking:

> We encourage students to support their statements with logical arguments, and to take responsibility for what they say. This helps them master the complexities associated with learning and speaking intelligently. Students are taught that they must be able to explain how they come to their conclusions. They must examine their thought processes, including their own preconceived notions and biases.

14. Make use of different student perspectives.

Students often value the opportunity to share their perspectives with each other. Find ways to incorporate differing reactions, beliefs, and perspectives. For example, use role-playing to portray alternative views. Ask students to represent certain groups whose perspectives have not surfaced. As Bubar and Vernon (2003, 159) write,

> Students who represent worldviews that differ from the majority challenge others to re-examine ... perspectives and ideas that most simply take for granted as true. All of our students seem to benefit from the introduction of other paradigms and diverse worldviews.

15. Seek closure.

When sensitive issues arise in class and disagreements arise, it can be very important to take time at the end to discuss what happened and reiterate certain principles and agreements. Plan to spend 10 minutes or so toward the end of class to process what happened, what was learned about the way that class unfolded, what changes need to be made in the future, etc.

Studies on memory show that a periodic focus on underlying concepts can reinforce a deeper learning. Schatz (2003, 130) writes:

> The last part of the discussion provides an opportunity for final summarization of key learnings that have emerged. During the last five to ten minutes of the group's time, it can also be helpful to ask if anyone has emotional 'rumblings.' ... In the ending stage, there also may be a need to restate the importance of retaining confidentiality about any self-disclosure that occurred.

16. Invite new thinking.

Change demands innovation. Without pretending to know all the answers, instructors can design their classes to explore a range of possibilities. We are all captives of limited experiences and belief systems. Revisit the ground rules you have for class and ask students to "stretch" to understand perspectives very different from their own. Helping our students ability to understand other viewpoints can promote the kinds of intellectual and emotional intelligence we value and need. Consider how Kreston (2003, 173-174) invites new thinking:

> I begin the course by explaining that my interest is to give students an opportunity to 'think' about disability differently. The students are invited to be open-minded and to contribute what they know from their own experiences, recognizing that each person may have a somewhat different familiarity with disability but a piece that can contribute to a more complete understanding.

17. Help students stretch.

At the end of a discussion in class, ask students to assess their own "stretching," how well they were able to understand the different perspectives expressed.

Bubar and Vernon (2003, 163-164) offer an example of helping their students stretch:

> By encouraging students to reach out beyond their own ethnocentricity and culture, beyond their own sense of worldview, we try to encourage students to develop a better understanding of each other. For example, when a student says she herself did not steal Native lands and does not see why tribes should have any right to get those lands back a hundred years later, we pose questions for the class about the ethics and values of our society, world opinion, and our own justice system. ... Regardless of how the colonials and Founding Fathers chose to act, we encourage our students to consider how legal decisions could have been decided, how society should conduct itself, and what values and morals we should advocate.

18. Require deeper analysis of experiences.

We enrich learning about diversity when we combine formal instruction with experiential assignments. If you use the latter, these assignments must be processed in a way that allows students to digest and benefit more fully from the experience. Following a class discussion, field trip, guest speaker, etc., have your students use the guidelines listed above to write about their experiences and reactions.

Val Middleton (2003, 109) offers the following guidelines to share with students: "(a) state your and/or your instructor's objectives for the activity/experience; (b) describe your participation in the activity; (c) personally react to the activity; (d) interpret the activity as it connects to the literature and other media (i.e., guest speakers, videos, novels, etc.); (e) apply the learning to your personal and professional responsibilities; (f) identify whether or not you met the original objectives and/or discovered any unforeseen outcomes; and (g) commit to a plan for improving future interactions with diverse others or diversity issues." According to Middleton, these guiding statements generally help students of diversity get into the flow of engaging in reflective activities in a structured or focused way while giving them the freedom to write about the experience in their own words.

19. Avoid easy answers and embrace complexity.

All too often, instructors reinforce dichotomous thinking by focusing too much on correct answers. It would be foolish for us to claim that there are simple answers to the complexities inherent in teaching about human diversity. Issues of diversity contain an overlapping of factors that requires some real sophistication to address. Consider what Suzanne Tochterman (2003, 143) recommends:

> When introducing new material, I frequently will remind my students of any competing theories, perspectives, interpretations, or ideas. All too often, they may otherwise be inclined to think that there is one final authority on some matter or another.

Support Student-Centered Learning

One way to move toward a pedagogy of human diversity is for instructors to embrace more student-centered learning, where the opportunities for personal reflection flow from interactions with others. Examples include journaling, course readings, instructor input, writing, guest speakers, films, individual and group assignments, and service learning projects.

20. Understand student development.

Learning about human diversity requires students to reflect honestly and openly on what they know, believe, and feel, the prejudices they need to unlearn, and the skills they will need to navigate our increasingly diverse and interdependent worlds. Accordingly, progress will be highly individualistic, a function of each student's background, motivation, openness, and ability.

As Canetto, Timpson, Borrayo, and Yang (2003, 290) note:

> For some students, especially those who are just starting to identify and affirm their own life meanings, this move from personal experience to critical analysis may be slow and difficult. Instructors also may find it useful to establish individual goals based on each student's development.

Reflect on a particularly challenging class session and re-evaluate the results based on an assessment of the developmental maturity of your students. Who responded well and who did not? Were there any surprises? What does this suggest about your plans for a future class session?

21. Challenge assumptions.

James Banning, who teaches in the School of Education at Colorado State University, offered the authors of this book two exercises for challenging the way that students think.

For the first activity, ask your students to identify as many associations as they can between animals and personality characteristics or behaviors. For example, "stubborn as an ox," "cute as a bug," "soft as a kitten," "brave as a lion," and so on. Record their contributions on the board. It usually takes about 15-30 minutes for the students to exhaust the possibilities. Then, ask the students which sex is usually associated with each of the animals listed. For example, in our culture we typically consider kittens as feminine, oxen as masculine, dogs as masculine, and so on. Once the class has assigned the label of masculine or feminine to each of the animals, then the personality/behavior characteristics associated with the animals can be summarized by sex. This exercise brings out the point that our culture has taught us stereotypical ways of viewing gender characteristics even in the simple descriptions of animal traits.

For the second activity, Banning reads the following list of colloquialisms and asks his students to shout out the words to fill in the blanks:

"Big boys don't _____."

"A woman's place is in the _____."

"Boys don't play with _____ ."

"Sugar and spice and everything nice: that's what little _____ are made of."

"Someday you'll meet Prince _____."

"Nice girls know how to keep their mouths _____."

"You should learn to take it like a _____."

"Nice guys finish _____."

"Boys don't like smart _____."

"Don't act like a _____."

"Boys will be _____."

You can then ask the students to generate additional sayings. The point of the exercise is that, despite the differences in backgrounds, the places the students have grown up, and their families, they all have learned the same cultural gender stereotypes of what boys and girls are "supposed" to be like.

This tip is not only about challenging the assumptions that your students make. You should also challenge your own assumptions.

While teaching a graduate course about diversity and special populations in rural Colorado, Angela Paccione (2003, 149) tried some opening activities to define terms like *race, racism, discrimination, oppression, ethnicity,* and *culture.* It didn't work. This class broke down into heated exchanges and emotional withdrawal. Rethinking that first class, Paccione realized that she had made some mistakes: "I had to suppress the urge to make assumptions about the students' readiness, closeness, openness, and experiences. I fell back on the basic triad that forms a foundation for diversity work: knowing self, knowing others, and making the connection."

Finally, reflect on a class session that went poorly and speculate about what would have been different if you had taken more time to unpack stereotypical thinking — both your students' and your own.

22. Encourage self-examination.

There is no substitute for self-reflection as a mechanism for finding a better alignment of values, beliefs, and actions. Experiment with a short reflective free-write in class as a prelude for a whole class discussion. You can then ask students to each share with a classmate nearby to see what they agree upon. You will be able to get everyone participating more once they have had this opportunity to prepare their thoughts and talk them through in a smaller, more intimate environment first. While difficult to assess objectively, reflective journals and open discussions can set the stage for deeper learning and transformation.

23. Use off-campus opportunities.

As ecologist and diversity trainer Nina Roberts (2003, 240) writes, experiences in the local community — for example, interviewing prominent citizens — can prove valuable for supplementing readings, lectures, and discussions and providing concrete references for various concepts under study. Have students brainstorm people they could interview who would bring different perspectives to the courses you teach. Make this a required activity and create time in class later in the semester for students to report back on their experiences.

24. Use student response sheets.

Find ways to allow students to ask those questions they will not ask in class, and respond to them in private until there is enough trust to bring these issues into the open for public discussion. Try the following activity that Roe Bubar (Bubar and Vernon, 2003, 161) uses with her students: pass a teacher/student response envelope around the classroom and encourage your students to ask about or comment on any issue from class. Then write a response to each question or concern.

25. Develop and use empathy.

Students often need help and support when wrestling with difficult ideas. Addressing racism, sexism, sexual orientation, class issues, and such will challenge them to face tough issues that have long divided cultures worldwide. Periodically stop a lecture or a discussion, whenever sharp differences of opinion or belief surface, and ask if students can really understand the perspective of someone who thinks that differently. Focus on how that person must feel, on developing empathy. Discuss that empathy is not the same as feeling sorry for someone. Feeling sorry for someone else, however well intentioned that reaction may be, can easily transform into pity and block a deeper understanding of those who are supposedly less fortunate.

Kreston (2003, 177) describes what she faces in her classes.

Unfortunately, the typical emotional response to disability seems to be rooted in sympathy, a 'feeling sorry for,' as opposed to empathy or an understanding of how someone might feel. The former tends to distance people while the latter tends to connect. One of the central goals of my class is to help students develop empathy for the disability experience, to understand it as a human condition and not an abnormality.

26. Build supportive classroom communities.

As a mechanism for reflecting on self, understanding individual uniqueness, and building a supportive community, experiment with expanded versions of the usual introductions in class. Have students bring something that really identifies them — a photograph they can pass around, a favorite stuffed animal that represents a special relationship, a ball cap of their favorite team. Ask them to emphasize three features of their identities: cultural, personal, and professional.

Here's an activity that Paccione (2003, 149) uses. "Students select a bag to carry artifacts that are representative of their identities. In the past these have included pictures, diplomas, tools of their trades, mementos, and heirlooms. Each student is given ten minutes to tell the group about the items in his or her 'people bag.' I always do the first one as a model." Pay attention to the potential benefits of the time invested in this kind of activity when you ask for responses to a question, spark a discussion, or begin a small group activity.

27. Connect to the personal.

Regularly look at the personal stories of individuals under study, their experiences, and their interests. This kind of research can help humanize any curriculum. But keep in mind that discussing the various "oppressions" of society can overwhelm students and cause them to become fatalistic, to think of themselves or others as hopeless victims.

Kreston (2003, 178) shares her strategies for keeping conversations regarding disability grounded in possibility.

Simply providing information about the ills of society may merely reinforce the perceived status (inferior) of disabled people through their 'struggle to overcome.' Yet, having a disability is both a personal experience as well as a societal one. A connection to that personal side is necessary if disability is to be perceived as part of the human condition and not deviant. The continuing challenge is to focus on the personal aspects of disability without further stigmatizing it.

28. Have students write a cultural autobiography.

Some students, despite their own varied and rich ethnic ancestries, may struggle to recognize the same strong heritage in other populations. When they research their own backgrounds, they may become more aware of diversity generally and open up new conversations about stories long buried under layers of neglect, ignorance, racism, and guilt.

Try the following. Jean Radin, a doctoral student in educational leadership and instructor in teacher licensure at Colorado State University, told the authors of this book how she has used "diversity paper dolls" as a creative approach for student autobiographies, with powerful results. Here's what she does.

Give each student a plain paper doll cutout, about 5-7 inches tall. These can be white or brown, as appropriate. Invite them to color their dolls to resemble themselves. When they have finished coloring, have them form small groups to discuss their accomplishments, honors, awards, etc.

Then break up the groups and have the students each tear off some part of his or her doll's body if he or she has had any of the following negative experiences. "If you have ever been the target of a racist, sexist, or homophobic slur or joke, then tear off .... If you have ever been with people who made racist or sexist jokes but you did not protest, then tear off .... If you have ever been afraid to walk in a certain area at night, then tear off ...." You can add more experiences that might relate to issues that have surfaced on your own campus.

When this is done, have students rebuild themselves by returning to accomplishments, skills, etc. and taping body parts back on. For example, "If you have you ever protested when someone told a racist, sexist, or homophobic joke, then tape on .... If you understand concepts like "white privilege" or "victimization" well enough to explain them to a classmate, then tape on ...."

After this rebuilding activity, students should write a short reflection, describing how they honestly felt about the activity and what this has meant to them personally.

29. Encourage participation and stir the soul.

Discussions will suffer if participation is limited to a few assertive students who dominate the conversation. Valuing wide participation and a range of ideas can help you find different ways to encourage quieter students and minority viewpoints to surface. In order to get more perspectives into class discussions, experiment with calling on students by name. Be sure to take a few minutes to get some feedback from both the entire class and individual students you get the chance to ask.

We can learn much from traditional American Indian practices that create open spaces for members to reflect and contribute without having to compete in the larger group for talk time. Roe Bubar and Irene Vernon (2003, 160, 161) write:

In many ways, we conduct class in the same manner that tribal groups have made important decisions. Open tribal meetings have been an integral part of tribal life from time immemorial .... We respectfully call on quiet students and provide small-group work to encourage the participation of those students who are reluctant to speak up in the larger classroom environment.

They then add:

We have also noticed that issues that come from the heart have been the ones that students are able to speak about with ease. When students are able to identify issues that stir their soul and consciousness, we find that their confidence to speak out increases.

30. Recognize the mix of the theoretical and the personal.

Developmentalists like Jean Piaget and Jerome Bruner have long argued for the importance of building theory from students' personal knowledge base, because abstractions are benefited by a foundation in experience. Explore the use of student journaling and how students are connecting course content with their own lives and beliefs. For example, Kreston (2003, 174) routinely asks students to draw on their own lived experiences as they study about disabilities.

I stress that I am not the sole authority and neither are the guest speakers. The whole of the disability experience is both theoretically based as well as personally perceived. Students are encouraged to contribute even if their perspectives may not seem to fit easily with others.

31. Allow time.

It usually takes time to reevaluate long and deeply held beliefs — beliefs that have developed and taken root over many years. Before completing an assignment, have students write a self-reflective *prologue* that addresses thoughts and feelings they bring to the assignment. Upon completing the assignment, ask them to include a self-reflective *epilogue,* noting any changes in their thoughts and feelings.

32. Emphasize constructivist learning.

Constructivism is a philosophy of learning based on the premise that we construct our understanding of the world through reflecting on our experiences. We each develop mental models and rules to make sense of our experiences; learning is the process of adjusting these models and rules to accommodate our new experiences.

Constructivism means two things to us as educators. First, that there is no knowledge independent of the meaning that the learner constructs from his or her experience; we do not absorb knowledge passively, but rather we develop it actively. Second, that when we think about learning, we must focus on the learner, not on the subject matter to be taught.

Unlearning dysfunctional biases while forming new concepts typically requires much more than is possible from a lecture- and information-based approach to instruction. Rethink an upcoming lecture or discussion topic that touches on some aspect of human diversity and frame it as a problem or case; this approach centers on the students, their discovery, their experiences. Ask students for feedback during your concluding summary. As part of your assessment, reflect on student learning and the quality of participation.

33. De-center authority — maybe.

Reflection and interaction are important when unlearning prejudice and learning about diversity. Experiment with shifting consciously from teacher-directed forms of instruction toward a more student-centered approach. Keep in mind that safety and openness may require a firm, guiding hand; there may be a fine line to walk here. Use student feedback and your own reflections about addressing diversity issues to help assess the impact.

As Canetto, Timpson, Borrayo, and Yang (2003, 287) caution:

One delicate issue in the engaged, diversity-content classroom has to do with the authority of the teacher. In many ways, these kinds of courses invite a de-centering of authority. On the other hand, the usefulness, feasibility, and process of de-centering oneself as an instructor may have to vary depending on one's personal characteristics, on institutional and systemic factors as well as on specific class dynamics.

Develop Rapport, Community, and Emotional Maturity

A pedagogy of human diversity also builds from an experience of shared learning, support, and commitment among students. In some sense, instructors can create an approximation of the ideal by transforming a class into a real community, where all members are able to address difficult, complex, and sensitive issues.

34. Find the positive in student responses.

It may require some real courage for students to address sensitive, emotionally charged diversity issues in the public classroom. Noticing the value in student contributions is one way to build confidence and promote more open and honest exchanges. Preface your comments on student papers by mentioning some of the positives you found in the paper, as well as any other things that you appreciate about the student, such as attendance and participation in class.

35. Get to know your students and make connections.

In the human hierarchy of needs set forth by Abraham Maslow (1959), maximal achievement requires some sense of safety and belonging. Joseph Lowman (1995) insists that the research on effective instruction in higher education points to two predominant factors — intellectual stimulation and instructor-student rapport.

Spend time helping your students get to know each other, in order to help build that sense of community that allows a more open, honest, and respectful discussion of sensitive diversity issues. Collect some biographical information from your students and look for ways to connect them with each other by interest or background. For example, in the spirit of building a sense of community in class, you could say, "I notice that Adriana likes to design Web sites. Who else shares that interest?"

Roe Bubar and Irene Vernon (2003, 159) describe how they promote a sense of community in their classes on Native American law and sovereignty:

> [On] the first day of class, we form a circle and fill out a personal questionnaire that helps students explore their unique experiences, hopes, and plans for the future. This is often a helpful way to start the class with an atmosphere of openness, introspection, sharing, and community. Because we tell the students that the personal questionnaire will be shared in the larger group, students can opt to share as much or as little as they feel comfortable doing. Once we know the composition of the class, we next want to begin creating an academic environment that is supportive, safe, and honest, one that will facilitate the study of law and cultural differences.

36. Make connections to student lives.

Take a few moments and write down your reflections on those classes in which you have been able to connect course content with the lives of your students. Make reminders to yourself to do something similar for upcoming topics.

With time, the most important connections may come most easily. As Angela Paccione (2003, 152) notes of one teaching experience, "I was able to make a human connection through my teaching style, my sense of humor, and my authenticity."

37. Support cooperation.

Rethinking stereotypes, unlearning prejudice, and developing new skills for this increasingly complex and interdependent world can be facilitated by interactions with thoughtful, encouraging teammates. Incorporate a small group activity into an upcoming topic or discussion. At its conclusion, ask for feedback from your students about the benefits of working together on course content.

For example, William Timpson (2003, 257) notes how "a group project allowed students to experience the benefits of a supportive team in addressing a challenging task," because of appropriate preparation.

With some background preparation on the requisite presocial skills (listening, empathy, consensus) as well as some understanding about the strengths and limitations of cooperative learning, several students noted how positive their experiences were. Without this kind of preparation, their experiences with teamwork in other classes had been mixed at best, often rife with frustration.

38. Teach students about emotional intelligence.

According to Timpson (2003, 18), "Gardner (1983, 1999) and Goleman (1994) both make compelling cases for including more attention to the emotional component of learning, especially where fear and resistance can play havoc with understanding more about diversity and about others who think differently."

The first researchers to use the term "emotional intelligence," Peter Salovey and John D. Mayer (1990), described it as "a form of social intelligence that involves the ability to monitor one's own and others' feelings and emotions, to discriminate among them, and to use this information to guide one's thinking and action." Later (1997) they refined their statement, defining emotional intelligence as the capacity to reason with emotion in four areas: to perceive it, to integrate it in thought, to understand it, and to manage it.

Use some debriefing time to check in with students about their reactions to open, honest, and respectful exchanges, what worked, what did not, and what is needed in the future. Explaining the basics of emotional intelligence can be an effective way to enter into a useful discussion about emotional intelligence in general and their experiences with it in learning.

39. Rearrange seating to facilitate interactions.

Large class sizes and rigid seating arrangements that force students to face forward limit the possibilities for the small group work that can promote more active, interactive, and deeper learning. Experiment with different seating arrangements and assess their impact on participation and classroom climate.

Nathalie Kees (2003, 58-59) describes how she will routinely rearrange seating:

If at all possible, I arrange the seating in the classroom in a circle or U-shape to facilitate student-to-student interaction and eye contact. At the beginning of the course, I tell students that I won't always be looking at them when they speak so that I can observe other students' reactions to what they are saying, draw other students into the conversation through eye contact, and encourage them to speak to each other rather than just to, or through, me as the instructor. If students continue to respond only to me, I will redirect them to the rest of the group through hand gestures and verbal cues.

40. Address guilt.

It is quite common for feelings of guilt about past injustices to shut students down, emotionally and intellectually, when classroom discussions focus on racial and ethnic diversity. Find an opportunity to put guilt on the table as a focus for analysis and class discussion. Begin with how you have handled your own feelings of guilt. Timothy Davies (2003, 49-50) describes how one administrator began to break through this barrier by first admitting her own guilt about doing too little to promote positive change. Finding the time, space, format, and support to have these kinds of heartfelt expressions of concern and self-disclosure can go far in building the trust, openness, and honesty needed to overcome guilt paralysis.

41. Share your own struggles.

Pick an upcoming topic, and begin class by recalling your earliest encounters with that material as a student — what was difficult for you to grasp, and what finally helped you to understand.

Raymond Yang (2003, 78) emphasizes that the instructor should be the first person to model self-disclosure:

> Instructors are the authoritative controllers of their classes; whatever they say is, virtually by definition, relevant. In this light, they can set an example for self-disclosure and convey a sense of openness by sharing personal information with their classes. This may be particularly beneficial when the information shared is obviously relevant to the material under study or leads students to link the material's meaning to their own experiences.

Kees (2003, 61) describes a situation in which she confronted a difficulty that many of us will face in sharing our struggles: "I wanted to use self-disclosure, but I didn't trust myself to stay in the role of leader of the group and not slip into a member role."

42. Help students understand systems.

We all live in systems that perpetuate and even promote biases — sexism, racism, heterosexism, ableism, ageism, classism, and others. Encourage your students do a deeper analysis of the systems they see that support particular policies or practices under study in your course.

43. De-emphasize evaluation during practice.

Experiment with having your students assess themselves in the run-up to an exam or deadline for a project. Have students submit an edited draft along with their finished paper and include a postscript comment about the changes they made based on the feedback they received.

Kees (2003, 58) has her students draw on criteria she has established to select their best performances (e.g., from among tape-recorded sessions of therapist/client interactions). She then grades the performance as "pass" or "redo" and provides specific feedback. This approach emphasizes meeting a set standard (mastery) rather than some norm-referenced evaluation based on an assumption of a normal distribution of grades.

Face Conflicts with Intelligence, Sensitivity, and Creativity

Disagreements, heated discussions, and tensions can be catalysts for growth as students confront issues of prejudice and bias, acceptance and appreciation. In the recommendations that follow, you will find some practical ideas for transforming conflicts into teachable moments that have the potential for lifelong benefits.

44. Discuss possible tensions.

Students' fear of misstatement can put a palpable chill on classroom discussions, but attempting to curry favor with instructors by telling them what they want to hear can only lead to mindless mimicry, intellectual dependency and emotional servitude. Identify a current issue that connects to an upcoming topic, and explore the range of reactions that students or others could have in contrast to any one supposedly "correct" response.

45. Know that there's a time to be objective and detached.

Reflect back on discussions about diversity topics. When have you felt *most* objective and detached? When have you felt *least* objective and detached? Make some reminders for yourself about upcoming topics. How can you be more objective and detached?

46. Counter polarization.

Learning requires that we be open and willing to move beyond defensiveness and rethink particular beliefs.

Recall a class in which your students became polarized. Make some notes about what you could have done differently, either to prevent or capitalize on this polarization. Plan to do something proactive for an upcoming class, such as sharing your concern about polarization and what ground rules everyone could agree to.

Roe Bubar and Irene Vernon (2003, 164) offer this advice when sides are forming:

> The class may devolve into standoffs between students of color versus whites, or women versus men, young versus old, and/or Native Americans versus others. If this type of polarization occurs, we reassert control over the class to ensure a classroom environment where everyone can speak about and explore the issues at hand. With open discussions, students can reflect on their own biases, understandings, and histories as well as the biases, understandings, and histories of others.

47. Prepare for sensitive topics.

Have your students write a few comments about times when they were hesitant to speak up in class. Ask them if they believe that shared readings and private reflections before the class discussion occurs would have helped. Plan to prepare differently for the next time a sensitive topic is scheduled for discussion.

In the aftermath of problems that surfaced in class around personal commitments to addressing diversity, Timothy Davies (2003, 51) describes how useful it was for him and his students to prepare for public discussions

> by leading into them with the readings and reacting to the readings through WebCT®'s electronic private mail journal, which is between the student and instructor. The students felt that, in this way, they could explore some of their thoughts and feelings in private before bringing them out to the cohort as a whole.

48. Remember that emotions can be constructive.

Strong emotions can be problematic in class — polarizing discussion, stifling open exchange, limiting honest reflection, and sparking anger, resentment, aggressiveness, and withdrawal.

Discuss the issue of emotion in class before beginning a sensitive topic. Come to some agreement about the ground rules you and your students want to follow. Assess the impact of the agreement and make any necessary modifications. You can also raise the issue after emotions have flared in class, analyze the effect on climate and learning, and come to some consensus about what to do differently.

Bubar and Vernon (2003, 163) describe how they channel anger when it arises. "As teachers, if we can control the climate in class, anger can be an acceptable emotion. However, anger must be directed in healthy ways that contribute to deeper learning. We must helps students direct their anger at the source of perceived problems — i.e., policy-makers — and not at each other."

Jane Kneller (2003, 219, 220-221) observes that "rational discourse has been culturally defined as excluding emotion and feeling, just as objectivity or distance in an argument have come to be seen as excluding, or at least taking prominence over, care and sympathy. This is especially true in the academy." She believes, however, that "it is important to make the discussion process less painful by setting up an environment in which there is no disgrace in occasionally breaking down emotionally, rambling, or simply losing the thread of a point a student is making. How the facilitator/teacher responds is crucial in guiding the responses of the rest of the class."

49. Explore possibilities with the performing arts.

With all its challenges and complexities, teaching about human diversity demands a certain degree of sophistication and creativity. Plan to experiment with more role-playing. Even more spontaneously, you can create a role-play, when during discussion, you feel there are strong views going unexpressed. Many students fear saying something in class that might upset someone else; assigning roles allows them to articulate positions that otherwise would remain unspoken. Remember that critical and creative thinking are enhanced when students are able to analyze and discuss different views.

Silvia Sara Canetto, William Timpson, Evelinn Borrayo, and Raymond Yang (2003, 282) make the following point: "Instructional approaches that tap into the rich possibilities of theater and psychodrama can be especially helpful when addressing diversity content and handling the range of reactions that can result. Role-playing, for example, can help students explore their reactions in simulated situations and practice alternative responses."

Unlearn Stereotyping and Prejudice

A pedagogy of human diversity may require the unlearning of old, dysfunctional, and problematic beliefs, attitudes, and values. Unfortunately, direct instruction may do little to change prejudices, dislikes, and hatreds that are deeply embedded in cultural histories, political power differences, regional enmities, income inequities, family traditions, and the like. Instructors will need to master a range of alternative approaches that go beyond surface knowledge and address a deeper understanding, awareness, and skill.

50. Discuss stereotypes.

Encourage your students to share their stereotypes of a particular group. This activity can be liberating, freeing them to speak the unspeakable, clear the air, and find new levels of honesty. The resulting cognitive dissonance can be a powerful catalyst for unlearning misconceptions, biases, and prejudices.

Start with a less sensitive category, such as height, college major, or favorite sports teams. Have students brainstorm both positive and negative stereotypes associated with a particular category. As students demonstrate some skill with this and seem comfortable, you can gradually raise the stakes and move into more sensitive categories, like religion, gender, and ethnicity. Finally, be sure to discuss the process itself and both the benefits and costs of this kind of open airing of stereotypes.

51. Recognize that there is no spokesperson for an entire population in your class.

It is quite common for a minority student to feel pressured to speak for all of his or her "group." Remember that there is always greater diversity within any group than ever exists between or among groups. You can help students who feel as if they are suddenly in the spotlight by noting that no one can ever be expected to speak for an entire population.

Try putting this issue of a "group spokesperson" on the table for discussion. Which generalizations are defensible, which are not, and how should they be expressed? For example, broadly speaking, is there a cultural tradition and expectation among Jewish and Asian peoples, groups commonly labeled in school circles as "model minorities," that especially value study and academic achievement? Or does the variability within these groups make this kind of assertion too simplistic to be of any real use? What disclaimers are necessary when discussing "group characteristics"?

52. Admit to your biases.

Fears about appearing racist or sexist in class can paralyze students who may have opinions, impressions, or questions that seem to reflect traditional stereotypes. If you model an honest openness, your example can give students one way to break out of old, dysfunctional patterns.

Mona Schatz (2003, 129) recommends introducing a personal bias you have — "something we believe or prefer but for which we have no factual justification" — with a phrase like "I know my bias will be evident when I say ...." Sharon Anderson, an associate professor in the School of Education at Colorado State University, provided the authors of this book with the following thoughts on self-disclosure:

> As a teacher, I struggle with how much to share myself, my real self, with students in a classroom setting. ... At times, I have been fairly open about my life experiences and at other times quiet. When it comes to differences, diversity, and understanding privilege, I think my students have felt freer to do self-exploration and share their lives when I have been more open about me, my life outside of the classroom, my struggles to understand my privilege as a white person, and my blunders as one who is still learning to listen to others who are different from myself. I don't always feel good about myself when I share my experiences (blunders and stereotypical thinking) and yet my sharing provides an example of genuineness and honesty that others (my students) may wish to follow and grow from.

53. Expose contradictions.

Find examples of dissonance in your field. Explore the various emotional dimensions involved. How could the dissonance be resolved in a constructive way?

Sometimes a desire to help and serve proves counterproductive to some degree, or even oppressive. Rosemary Kreston (2003, 174) often finds herself guiding students to face what may be problematic and stereotypical about their choice of a "helping career." However difficult the resulting re-evaluation, exposing these contradictions may be the best way to help her students move toward a more functional belief system.

> Their feelings of wanting to 'give to' and 'help' others may be the primary motivation for their career choice. It may be difficult to accept that one's kind-hearted efforts to help another who is less fortunate (less able) could be seen as oppressive. Understanding oppression based on kindness can create a great deal of dissonance, both intellectually and emotionally.

54. Understand privilege.

Help the students discuss the privileges enjoyed by various groups of people. You could start with "white privilege" — "those unspoken, unwritten rules of conduct by which Whites are treated by others," usually including the "freedom to select any place to live, to shop without being followed, to write checks without showing identification, to secure bank loans with no collateral, and to be offered employment on the basis of one's family or friends rather than one's resume" (Paccione 2003, 151). Allow students to explore its various implications, i.e., historical, economic, educational, social, even personal and emotional. You could also explore the implications of "social class privilege" or "majority privilege."

55. Critically examine the standard or ideal.

Understanding diversity cannot be just a study of those who have been marginalized, segregated, ostracized, oppressed, exploited, or ignored. The other side of any equation for reform must address the values, attitudes, beliefs, and behaviors of those with power, status, resources, and privilege. Teaching about diversity "also means including a critical examination of the experiences of all of those who have been implicitly presented as the standard or ideal in the academic canon, including men, the upper class, and people from industrialized countries" (Canetto, Timpson, Borrayo, and Yang 2003, 276).

Explore with your students what would constitute the ideal representative of your field, and discuss the assumptions behind that assessment. Do disciplinary leaders reflect mainstream sentiments? What is the prevailing paradigm about diversity issues in your field? Does the embrace of that paradigm determine who gets published and what gets taught?

56. Speak the truth and name the oppression.

Although challenging, it is important for instructors to help students learn how to face injustice, past and present, how to understand pain and suffering, what our ethical responsibilities are, and how healing can happen. The language and the concepts we use can have a powerful effect on learning, organizing what we read and hear into categories.

Help your students identify problems in your area of study — what "truths" need to be explored and what "oppressions" need to be identified. Offer resources in your field that focus on efforts to name and confront oppressions, along with the stories of individuals involved. Take time to assess the impact of this kind of discussion.

How liberating is it to publicly state what typically only a few radical types dare to say?

For example, Bubar and Vernon (2003, 156) describe what they face when addressing the history of law and policies for Native Americans in the United States: "We focus on how Indian nations in this country never have been afforded the ability to assert their sovereignty in its fullest extent within the confines of the judicial system. ... In the face of this kind of (in)justice, it becomes a real challenge for us to get students to learn this history and to then empower them to think about the law in a more ethical and equitable manner." For example, how do we internally frame the idea of Christopher Columbus if we call him an "explorer" or label him an "emissary" for European imperialists greedy for the resources of the new world. Or, given the resulting deaths of millions of Native peoples, could we judge him guilty of war crimes and genocide?

Here's another example. Kreston (2003, 171) teaches about the terrible abuse that disabled people have historically suffered.

Society's response to disability (as deviant) has ranged from such atrocities as infanticide and the holocaust ... to relatively benign habits of designing facilities with only one accessible restroom per floor or protesting group homes in neighborhoods. As a result, people with disabilities have experienced systematic oppression, discrimination, isolation, and devaluation from those who are non-disabled.

57. Have courage.

Model for your students a process in which we explore our own prejudices in the very public space of the classroom and then open up to new thinking. Think of the challenging experiences you have had in class around issues of diversity, such as angry outbursts or tearful responses. Assess your courage in handling what occurred. Make plans on how best to handle those same situations in the future.

As Canetto, Timpson, Borrayo, and Yang (2003, 288) conclude in *Teaching Diversity*: "This is admittedly complex terrain to navigate and requires understanding, skill, clarity, and courage on everyone's part."

Create Safe, Open, Inclusive, and Supportive Classrooms

Research on school climate has identified several factors (determinants) that help to boost student morale and encourage deeper learning. The ideas that follow represent a range of practical and creative ideas for attending to all those "process" factors (communication, cooperation, values, attitudes, beliefs) that can be especially important when taking on the sensitive issues associated with human diversity.

58. Balance openness and safety.

The value of free and open interactions needs to be balanced against the requirements for safety. A positive classroom climate enables students to discuss and challenge ideas without fear of personal attack by other students or retaliation by an instructor whose biases affect the grades given. Everyone should be heard and differences should be accepted while the students and instructor are probing the cohesiveness of underlying arguments. As part of a discussion about ground rules in class, encourage your students to help you define what "openness" and "safety" mean for them and their learning.

Silvia Sara Canetto, William Timpson, Evelinn Borrayo, and Raymond Yang (2003, 277-278) note:

> Creating an open and safe classroom involves a complicated and sometimes contradictory set of actions .... Openness may mean allowing a spontaneous flow of contributions: safety, however, may involve managing the traffic of contributions so that there is a diversity of speakers who won't fear retaliation.

59. Encourage participation.

Citing *Women's Ways of Knowing: The Development of Self, Voice, and Mind* (Belenky, Clinchy, Goldberger, and Tarule 1986), Timpson (2003, 17) contends that

> it becomes important for instructors to encourage participation in classroom discussions because it is in this way that students, ... 'find their voices' and mature intellectually. Early on in this process, acceptance of contributions without harsh judgment can be important for learning and development.

Use gestures and eye contact to encourage participation from your students, as Kees describes (see page 37).

Try polling to assess reactions generally — "How many of you agree with that last point? How many disagree? How many are unsure?" Then, call on specific students to elaborate.

Remember that students learn best when they feel safe to participate fully and learn much from their explorations and mistakes. Every student should feel included, supported, and validated. Knowing the classroom norms and expectations needed for respectful interactions helps to set that foundation.

60. Ensure care when speaking.

Addressing sensitive and complex issues, whether face to face in a classroom or at a distance on an electronic discussion board, requires some skill and understanding on everyone's part.

As part of an exercise, ask students to define and evaluate certain words that were used during a discussion. Were there better choices? What else needs to be said when, for example, words like "racist," "sexist," "homophobic," and "victimization" are thrown around?

Bubar and Vernon (2003, 166) emphasize certain principles for classroom discourse. "We teach students that they must be careful with their words: they must claim them and take responsibility for them. For us, 'political correctness' in the classroom demands respectful language and active listening so that we can challenge ideas and not the person."

61. Use student dyads.

Pairing students in class can create a relatively safe forum for discussing sensitive matters involving personal feelings or perceived threats and injustice. In effective dyads, students may be more likely to offer honest reactions and explore deeper insights.

Redesign an upcoming class to incorporate the use of dyads for exploring some aspect of diversity. Provide clear expectations of what you want and in what amount of time. Monitor the quality of these interactions, either by observing from the front or moving around the room and listening in. Make a point to assess the value of this approach. Ask students what worked and what could be improved.

62. Practice generosity.

Addressing the legacies of racism, sexism, homophobia, and other forms of discrimination can churn up hard feelings that strain classroom discussions and relationships. Suzanne Tochterman (2003, 142) describes one reference she uses to sustain a positive, constructive focus: *Reclaiming Youth at Risk: Our Hope for the Future,* by Larry Brendtro, Martin Brokenleg, and Steve Van Bockern (1990). In it the authors discuss

> empowering students through a focus on values traditionally associated with Native American culture. They stress the importance of communal interdependence and collective learning .... This Native American approach considers generosity to be one of the greatest virtues. The authors want school to move from alienation to belonging, from inadequacy to mastery, from egoism to generosity. These values can be the unifying themes for a positive school culture. ... Meeting students where they are and providing environments in which all young people can grow and flourish are ... core values.

Generosity, according to Brokenleg, is basically "the natural human need to be a good person, ... to contribute to the community." Reflect back on your teaching and ask yourself how you could have been more generous without artificially inflating grades, how you could have built a greater sense of belonging and mastery. Rethink your upcoming classes and plan to experiment with some changes in this direction.

63. Create alliances and contracts with students.

Students can feel suddenly and surprisingly alone among their classmates, such as when they make a comment and nobody reacts. You can support a student who may feel embarrassed and isolated by incorporating the comment, by saying, for example, "You know, that happened to me, too" or "I can remember feeling that way once." In this way, you can separate the point from the student and become an ally. To the extent that the comment is on point, you can then invite the other students to analyze it: "So, there are at least a couple of us who .... So, let's take a look at it."

To encourage all of her students to participate, Jane Kneller (2003, 221) shares anecdotes about her own experience as an undergraduate who kept quiet in class "for fear of sounding stupid or saying the wrong thing." She notes, "Typically they find this astonishing and want to know what happened and how that changed." Then some of her most timid students are more willing to open up in class or ask her for advice on how to overcome similar fears.

To help codify these alliances, you can develop concrete agreements and post them in the classroom to force an attention to the language and reality of inclusiveness, to remind your students how mutual respect, honesty, and sensitivity can be phrased as expectations about discussions, questions, responses, relationships, etc.

Mona Schatz (2003, 127-128) notes:

Often, when I ask students to build a contract — a conscious agreement for the learning in this class — they will stare at me, befuddled. I have to start with some basic suggestions such as 'we will all respect each other's opinions' and 'everyone must listen respectfully.' Once I help students see that we are creating a safe learning environment with this kind of contracting process, they start to introduce ideas that are important to them.

Reflect back on alliances you have successfully created in your classes. Where have you failed? Ask your current students to suggest ways to nurture constructive alliances in your class. What ground rules can everyone agree to?

64. Practice democracy and promote citizenship.

Model in the classroom what is needed from citizens in a democracy: acceptance, tolerance, critical thinking, and cooperation. Take opportunities to emphasize listening as a skill for learning and living in a democracy. Show your students how accepting responsibility for a group project can help balance the divisive competition that characterizes too many classrooms and can reinforce an important component of citizenship. Encourage your students to identify opportunities in the larger community where they could get involved in issues related to the content of your course.

Bubar and Vernon (2003, 165) connect active learning and student empowerment within the larger framework of democratic citizenship: "Empowerment comes in a variety of ways. We think it is imperative for students to recognize their rights, how precarious those rights may be, and how easily they can be taken away. Another way to build student empowerment is to encourage them to speak out at public meetings and represent themselves and others effectively."

65. Be humble.

Reflect on your own abilities to help students learn, listing both strengths and vulnerabilities. Identify those areas of professional growth that would help you develop the additional skills you may need.

Consider this experience, related by Timothy Davies (2003, 51):

In class, when I changed my behavior from the 'safety' of lecturing to a more vulnerable role as facilitator, helping students to construct their own knowledge, I began to realize what true humility is for me. The responsibility of helping create a learning environment that not only feels safe but is safe is a far more complex task than preparing a lecture ever was for me. Facilitation of learning is more demanding and risky for me than preparing a lecture.

66. Develop student leadership skills.

Learning is always a shared journey. The more you can help students develop the skills they need to communicate effectively, the more they are willing to assume greater responsibility for their own learning and the more likely they can learn the lessons of diversity.

Spend some time early in the semester drafting ground rules about effective, open, and respectful communication. How can you encourage your students to be more responsible for their own learning? Periodically revisit these rules, assess what has occurred in class since you adopted them, and consider any modifications needed. These ground rules form a foundation for student community leadership.

67. Honor choices.

When addressing diversity issues, students often feel at least somewhat unsure how to address members of various groups. While norms can shift over time, individuals can still assert their own individual preferences and reasonably expect others to honor their wishes. It's all in the process of how these norms, expectations, and responses are played out, whether with anger and fear or sensitivity and acceptance. Because no one can ever be certain if or what someone else wants to be "labeled," it is important for instructors to establish guidelines that allow for feedback and corrections, and honor the choices students make. Have your students reflect on the terms they would prefer for themselves and come to an agreement about how best to correct someone who uses an inappropriate or undesired term.

68. Insist on responsible language.

One fundamental ground rule for a safe environment that all members of the class community — instructor and students alike — respond to each other with understanding and empathy, especially when there are sharp disagreements.

Reexamine the language used in a particular class that dealt with some aspect of diversity. For the purposes of expressing and discussing more precisely, consider the impact of alternative language — terms, concepts, qualifying adjectives and adverbs — that could have been used.

69. Ensure safety for instructors.

Diversity content can spark enough discomfort for some students to conclude that there is a problem with their instructor, the content, and/or the course design: "problems of safety may ... arise as students turn their negative reactions about a difficult and painful learning process against their teachers" (Canetto, Timpson, Borrayo, and Yang, 2003, 279). For example, raising questions about "privilege" has caused some students to believe that their instructor had a "liberal bias," was engineering some kind of "guilt induction" for past sins, and was demanding a "politically correct" line of reasoning.

Take a few moments and reflect on the safety you feel — or don't feel — in your department and on your campus when it comes to teaching about human diversity. Is there any appreciation for the special challenges of teaching this kind of course, such as how lower student course evaluations may reflect the inherently more emotionally challenging nature of the content?

While departments are working toward uniform systems for evaluating teaching, it is important for all faculty members and administrators to recognize the special challenges for anyone who agrees to teach these courses. As Canetto, Timpson, Borrayo, and Yang (2003, 280) conclude, "Being in a 'safe' department can be especially important for anyone teaching diversity content. In this case, a safe department means a department that is aware of the complexities of teaching about diversity and does not automatically assume that one's teaching difficulties are a sign of insufficient effort, incompetence, lack of openness to students' feedback, or human diversity biases."

70. Reduce perceived threat.

Students may feel uncomfortable discussing sensitive issues related to diversity. Instructors should be attentive to their feelings and reduce any feelings of risk.

You reduce perceived threat when, for example, you don't chide a student who makes a clearly ignorant or insensitive comment; instead, you find some positive aspect of it and consider only that part as the contribution. If a student makes a comment that seems beyond redemption, simply thank him or her for at least being willing to say something (e.g., to "break the ice") and move on.

Identify three or so incidents from previous classes when students said things related to diversity that created some tension or led to a misunderstanding. Evaluate how you handled each situation. Make plans for handling similar situations in future classes.

71. Create supportive policies and practices.

As is true for most campus changes, energized leaders and new resources will be needed to support a deeper institutional commitment to diversity and to improve classroom instruction.

Evaluate the support for diversity generally on your campus and for improvement and innovation in teaching. Identify strategies for linking diversity and instructional improvement. Find allies. Draft a brief position paper and submit it to various campus leaders for comment.

In their conclusion to *Teaching Diversity,* Canetto, Timpson, Borrayo, and Yang (2003, 281) arrive at the following recommendation: "One thing is sure: No class is an island. What happens in a diversity-content class in terms of openness and safety is influenced by department and university values, attitudes, policies, and evaluation and reward practices. Thus, one recommendation is that departments and institutions develop forms of teaching support and evaluation that address the specific skills, tasks, and demands created by diversity-content teaching."

Develop Your Instructional Skills

Without any serious campus attention to teaching and professional development, the complexities, sensitivities, and interdisciplinary nature of human diversity content will challenge a traditional university focus on disciplinary knowledge and research. In the tips that follow, instructors will find many ideas that can help them address ethnicity, gender, social class, homophobia, and a range of other diversity issues in class. These suggestions should also help them improve their teaching generally, encouraging better communication and deeper learning.

72. Manage multiple roles and use varied approaches.

Because diversity issues strike so many chords in people, intellectually and emotionally, instructors need to be flexible to meet the different needs of their students. Create an inventory of the varied approaches you have used when addressing diversity issues. As you assess the effectiveness of each, make reminders for yourself about upcoming classes and topics.

Mona Schatz (2003, 129-130) frames it as a commitment to different approaches: "Using varied learning strategies such as dyads and triads also can help students build confidence as discussants. Short video or movie clips or news stories can be useful as jumping-off points. They can portray some issues quickly and allow students to engage fully in a topic that may be difficult to introduce otherwise. By using case studies — for example, a depiction of someone who is harassed in the workplace — you can externalize a sensitive topic and provide a useful concrete context."

73. Use simulations.

Simulations are approximations to the "real world" that can provide active, engaging, shared, and concrete experiences to support the learning of various concepts or theories. For example, having students wear blindfolds can help them "see" what the loss of sight can mean for navigating the world.

Reflect on simulations you have led or experienced as a participant. Identify their strengths. How could you compensate for their weaknesses? Select or design a simulation for an upcoming class topic. For ideas, search the Web using as key words "simulations" and "teaching diversity." Learn from colleagues around the country and the world.

74. Model what you expect.

Using the skills that you want students to develop — for example, making sensitive, honest and respectful responses — can provide a powerful demonstration of what you are teaching and what they read. It can be a powerful mechanism for building a positive and honest classroom community Consider what Mona Schatz (2003, 129) says about modeling: "Modeling what we expect seems self-explanatory. It really is not. Modeling appreciation for the contributions of another person may not be something that an instructor is used to doing. Saying 'thank you for sharing your own ideas and experiences' indicates to students a sense of your genuine regard. ... I myself have said, 'What you have described is very interesting — information I was not aware of before."

Assess the modeling you have done in class before. What seems to have worked? How could you improve? What will you commit to doing in future classes?

As Schatz reflects: "If instructors are uncomfortable talking about their experiences with discrimination, it is less likely that students will be willing to talk about their own experiences. We can help students by disclosing our own discomforts, ambivalences, and concerns when talking about sensitive topic areas."

75. Understand and use your own reactions.

Katherine Allen (1995, 140) recommends journaling to increase self-awareness:

> Making use of a teaching diary ... allows an instructor to debrief from intense classroom experiences and provides a written record of what happens in class. Over time, a teaching diary can become the basis for reflection about effective teaching strate-

gies as well as documentation of the teacher's growth and empowerment.

Keep a teaching journal: make notes about how you are reacting in class and sharing your feelings with your students. Note also the benefits that you perceive in your reactions and draw up plans for future classes.

76. Connect teaching and learning.

The best classes contain a dynamic relationship between instructors and students whereby experiences are shared, inspected, analyzed and evaluated. Teaching about diversity adds other layers of complexity as the identities of instructors and students alike can be factored into lessons and analyzed.

Solicit periodic feedback from students at the end of class to better connect teaching and learning. Take a few minutes to ask them, for example, to write down one thing that went well in class that day, one are of possible confusion and one idea for an improvement. Read and respond at the next class session. You could also do this more formally and more extensively at mid-semester, even using a colleague to facilitate so that students feel more free to be honest and forthcoming.

77. Be enthusiastic about teaching.

Students at all levels and across all disciplines routinely identify the instructor's enthusiasm for the subject as important to them and their motivation for learning. When teaching about diversity, however, there is a layer of complexity and sensitivity that can be problematic when students connect an instructor's passion with proselytizing and worry that any disagreements could mean a lower grade, further inhibiting those already anxious about speaking out on anything controversial.

Evaluate your own energy levels for teaching. When are they highest? Lowest? What makes the difference? Make plans for keeping your energies high in future classes. Monitor the impact on yourself and your teaching.

Rosemary Kreston (2003, 183) offers the following insight into teaching effectively: "I have come to realize ... that whether or not I am a 'good' instructor may not be as important as being enthusiastic about and engaged with what I am teaching."

78. Use course web sites.

A Web site on which you and your students can post reflections and react to what others have written allows you to extend classroom discussions and permits greater participation. A Web site generally empowers students and is especially helpful for involving quieter, more reflective students. If you include postings as part of a participation grade, you can reward engagement through formal assessment.

Check with colleagues who make regular use of Web-based programs like WebCT® to support their courses. What do they say about the impact of a course Web site on participation and reflection?

79. Solicit feedback from students always and in all ways.

Success with diversity content courses often hinges on communication, the degree to which instructors and students can navigate the complexities and sensitivities that surround issues that touch on ethnicity, gender, sexual orientation, religion, social class, and so forth. Ask your students from time to time about their learning, what is helping, where there might be problems, and what ideas they might have for improvement.

You can also make a commitment to get to class a few minutes early and check with a few students about their reactions to previous class topics, assignments that are coming due, a guest speaker, or whatever.

Canetto, Timpson, Borrayo, and Yang (2003, 282) suggest recruiting a colleague to conduct "interviews, focus groups, a survey, or a formal mid-semester student feedback session" to encourage students to express any fears, concerns, appreciations, and recommendations early enough to make changes. They add, "Perhaps as important, everyone is challenged to see teaching and learning as a shared, co-created process."

80. Teach from the heart.

Afford some time and space in your teaching routine to follow your instincts and to grab on to those "teachable moments." Take time in and out of class to assess the impact of such moments against that of straight content coverage.

Bubar and Vernon (2003, 160) describe how they make these connections:

As Native women, we agree that much of our teaching is from the heart, a process whereby both teachers and students learn together .... We try to overturn what we term 'academic distance.' ...When teachers are content to simply lecture, there is no acknowledgment that the students and their interactions with one another merit any academic value.

81. Invite diverse guests.

Review your upcoming course topics and think about including resource people who represent diverse backgrounds and could add some different perspectives and undermine your students' assumptions and stereotypes. Guests can connect with your students on a very personal level; moreover, students will usually value the variety of experiences and the thoughts and feelings that a resource person can share.

82. Assign journals.

Experiment with occasional reflective free-writes in class, allowing students a little time and quiet to collect their thoughts into something coherent. Consider requiring a journal for a particular course in which ongoing reflections could be an important mechanism for stimulating deeper learning.

The students may benefit greatly from keeping a journal of their reactions and reflections on class discussions, assigned readings, and other relevant experiences or opinions they feel like sharing. These can serve as reminders about key concepts, express confusion, raise questions that need to be addressed, and provide starting points for deeper exploration.

83. Make teaching transparent.

Take some time to think back over your teaching experiences, and succinctly describe your teaching style. Experiment with including this description in your course syllabus, taking a few minutes to discuss it in class. Challenge your students to understand their own reactions to what you do in comparison with what other instructors do. This degree of transparency will help promote self-awareness and honesty, both of which are vital to the study of human differences.

Every instructor develops a unique style of teaching, connecting the various techniques, activities, or practices that he or she employs during a course. Students may or may not appreciate your style, independent of the course content. Understand your teaching style and let students in on your choices, to help them adapt and avoid unnecessary frustration. When you model self-awareness in this way, you can also help your students reflect on and understand their own reactions.

84. Evaluate your course with your students.

Draw on course evaluations to improve your course and your teaching strategies and techniques. But don't wait until it's over. In addition to the usual evaluation at the end of the term, Timpson (2003, 16) recommends a mid-course evaluation as being valuable for the students as well as for the instructor: "One benefit of mid-semester course evaluations is to promote the kind of meta-cognitive awareness — i.e., thinking about thinking ... that can permit students to reflect more deeply about their experiences as learners and better understand their own reactions to complex and challenging material."

Communicate and Collaborate

When the material under study becomes emotionally overwhelming and tensions arise in the classroom, fostering open communication and productive teamwork can reduce anxiety to a level at which the entire class is comfortable.

85. Emphasize collaboration and prosocial skills.

Make an inventory of the kinds of prosocial skills — listening, communications, negotiating — that could enhance learning in your class, especially for those group projects or interactive exercises that can begin to bridge differences that otherwise separate students. Collaboration toward a common goal is perhaps the most powerful mechanism for increasing acceptance and improving attitudes generally.

Although instructors can feel intense pressure to cover specific content, developing the communication skills that underlie collaboration can prove well worth the effort in the long run. Effective teamwork can enhance learning both within a course and in the world beyond. Timpson (2003, 16) notes:

> The literature on cooperative learning ... describes various prosocial skills that students need to work successfully in groups .... We now know that the communication skills and group dynamics so important in today's world, from listening to empathy and consensus, can be taught and learned.

Along with establishing ground rules for respectful communication, building a positive climate also means creating the kind of peer support that helps students open up to other viewpoints and rethink their own beliefs. It's important for students to feel a sense of belonging, something often neglected in the push to cover content.

86. Practice professionalism.

Another way to encourage respectful communication and interactions is to teach and expect "professional" behavior. Make a list of those "professional" skills and attitudes that are essential in your field. Consider how you could incorporate more of these into your classes.

Professionalism can be modeled, for example, in courtroom decorum, where certain rules and practices help mediate even the most difficult, sensitive, or inflammatory of cases. Bubar and Vernon (2003, 166) describe what they do in their own classes:

> We believe that respectful language, in conjunction with professionalism, builds knowledge and student skills. For example, Roe provides a moot court experience as a significant part of the course. She has incorporated an oral argument requirement, and she prepares students in a more traditional legal setting. In some ways, this class activity is grounded in traditional Native teachings that emphasize preparation through practicing arguments and watching others.

87. Prize relationships.

Design cooperative assignments that foster positive interdependence. It can be especially important to be proactive and invest some time during the semester helping groups work together more successfully.

Build in periodic opportunities for your students to recognize and thank each other. Encourage them to applaud after a presentation or a group report. Use holidays from different traditions as well as the end of the semester to stop, reflect, and recognize the special contributions that people have made both in class and in the larger community.

88. Balance participation.

Some students participate very actively, while others participate little or not at all. Plan ways in which you can respectfully limit the participation of dominating students while drawing out more from those who have said little.

One way to accomplish this is to discuss the issue in class and come up with new ground rules, e.g., "Be sure that no one else wants to contribute before commenting another time." Another is to talk with your students individually, outside of class. This can be as important for the confident student who participates easily and often as for the insecure introvert who would rather hide!

Kneller (2003, 221-222) writes about how she deals with both:

Nearly every year, in at least one of my classes, I have an overly vocal student whom I ask to meet with briefly after class. I give this student heartfelt thanks for his or her many contributions, and explain that if I cut him or her off or don't call on him or her it's simply because I want everyone to have the chance to speak, and that I want everyone to have the benefit of hearing all their classmates' views. ... For the timid or quiet student who wants to speak but has trouble, I find that very concrete suggestions help. My colleagues in speech communication have shared with me all sorts of tricks for overcoming stage fright, and I try to pass these on to students. In some cases I have simply referred them to a good beginning speech class.

89. Acknowledge group support and build teamwork.

Take some class time to go beyond the usual quick introductions, for example, and learn something about each student's background, likes, and dislikes. As a refresher at the start of the next class, ask students to reintroduce themselves and describe their favorite dessert, or to choose a vehicle that would represent them and explain why. This can be much fun! More importantly, this kind of activity can go far toward building a sense of community that in turn can support greater participation, risk taking, and learning.

Davies (2003, 50) describes a situation where 14 doctoral students who had gone through a negative experience in their distance learning course requested more team-building exercises so that they would feel better equipped to address deep and difficult issues of diversity that were barriers for their individual and collective progress. Mona Schatz (2003, 130) notes, "As the discussion process unfolds, I have ... found it essential to acknowledge the support that group members are giving to each other. In this way, I can work toward a shared group management of the learning process."

90. Be credible.

All too often, opinions and personal experiences dominate discussions about diversity. A cloud of emotions can then hang over a classroom and put a chill on open, honest, and informed exchanges. Being very aware of what you say and the sources you cite can increase your credibility for your students.

Kreston (2003, 169) writes of the self-discipline she has developed in teaching:

As with other diversity instructors, the acceptance of my authority is highly influenced by how I present myself and how I am received. While self-disclosure is integral to teaching about the disability experience, I have to be careful to ensure that specific information does not become interpreted only as an opinion and, therefore, invalidated.

Put reminders in the margins of your class notes to differentiate between personal opinion and those assertions that have some support in published research. Discuss the value of this awareness, how it can be maintained, and how people can support each other's honesty.

91. Use student legacies.

As instructors, we make a concerted effort to develop a classroom climate that allows for open, honest, and respectful communication, and when that happens, we take some satisfaction. Yet when the semester ends and those students move on, we have to start all over again with another group of students!

Are there ways to capture some of those student legacies for future classes? Think about how you could capture some of the wisdom of current students for future use. For example, you could videotape group presentations and use the best ones as models. You could also keep exemplary papers and reports — but be sure to get signed and dated student agreements about using their work in this manner.

Davies (2003, 53) describes ways in which his doctoral program in Community College Leadership attempts to use advanced students and graduates to help advise, support, and assist each new cohort.

As these new doctoral students follow the advice of the doctoral class that went before, they acknowledge their predecessors' wisdom and see the results. Then, understanding the value of this culture and climate, this new group can add its own wisdom as their legacy to those who will follow in their footsteps. In this process of helping students learn, there is no conclusion — only a commencement.

92. Make use of classroom diversity.

Your students can be a tremendous resource for teaching about diversity. Look for ways that the experiences, beliefs, and backgrounds of each of them can help the others better connect concepts under study. If you have students complete an inventory of their experiences at the start of a semester, you'll have ideas about whom to tap and for which topics. Assigning reflective papers will give you many more ways that you can draw students into class discussions.

Note how Bubar and Vernon (2003, 158) make use of their students in their Federal Indian Law and Policy course:

> In our experience, students of color, women, gays, lesbians, bisexuals, transgendered students, and students with disabilities often will have more experience with cultural oppression. Thus their participation can add much to understanding what it means to be marginalized. ... Informed of Native issues and concerns, they can add their own experiences with oppression.

93. Teach and practice I-messages.

Nathalie Kees (2003, 58) describes how she gets students to express their differing opinions without fear of criticism or retaliation. They use I-statements — "I believe ...," "I think...," "From my viewpoint...," "I'm feeling ...." I-statements require them to take personal responsibility for what they say, to label it as their opinion and feeling and not a fact or some universal truth. The use of I-statements also discourages students from playing the devil's advocate and hiding their own beliefs. At times, Kees will cut off students and ask them to rephrase generalizations into "I think/feel" statements. "'I-statements' help us disagree with what has been said rather than argue with the person who has made the statement."

Draw on your experiences in previous semesters to create a few case studies so that students can practice I-messages, i.e.

Challenge Ideas, Attitudes, and Beliefs

Fundamental to a pedagogy of human diversity is the challenge for instructors of shifting from a preoccupation with the transfer of knowledge to inclusion of approaches that allow students to explore possibilities. If we only pass on the traditions, beliefs, values, and assumptions of the dominant culture, how do we question the underpinnings of prejudice toward any other perspective?

94. Challenge traditions and question basic concepts.

Every discipline is embedded in certain ways of thinking that it's leading authorities generally support but which others question and challenge. The same is true for diversity. Recognizing when particular ideas are no longer useful has long been a benchmark for a mature, independent thinker.

Examining the barriers to greater acceptance and tolerance often means confronting the very ways we think. Make a list of some basic assumptions in your courses, the prevailing paradigms. Identify what the assumptions and paradigms that had been in vogue earlier. Discuss with students what current ideas might shift in the near or distant future.

Here's an example of challenging traditions and questioning basic concepts from Rosemary Kreston (2003, 169, 173), the director of a university unit that serves disabled and special needs students:

> I believe that, when taught from a perspective outside the more established [medical] viewpoint, a study of disability lends itself well to diversity curricula in several ways. However, this perspective is also one that challenges the traditional underpinnings of several 'helping' professions and, hence, challenges many students.

Kreston challenges her students to look deeply at the assumptions that guide their deepest beliefs and motivations about their desire to work with disabled people.

What often is unexamined is how the pathological perspective (disability as deficit) continues to perpetuate isolation and separateness (for people with disabilities). Students who enroll in my class are required to examine their perceptions as well as question concepts they may have taken for granted. It can be quite a shock to realize one's career choice is to join a system that, under the guise of support, may add to an imposed isolation.

95. Value diverse perspectives.

Discussions can be richer when students are willing to share different and unique viewpoints.

Explain the value of different perspectives in sparking better and more creative decisions, for example. Experiment with role-playing to surface unique viewpoints.

When they are successful in this regard as instructors, Roe Bubar and Irene Vernon (2003, 154) believe that their students "leave [their] classes challenged, reflective, and oftentimes more aware of the different human and cultural issues around them."

96. Address taboo subjects.

In a misguided commitment to classroom safety that can only undermine a deeper learning, instructors may avoid certain difficult issues in order to preserve a more comfortable environment. Addressing diversity issues invariably means introducing some degree of tension in a course.

Use a "fishbowl" technique to address a sensitive topic on diversity. While an inner circle discusses the issue, everyone else takes notes on the interaction. The students then share their observations and explore various ways of handling this kind of sensitive material.

For example, Bubar and Vernon (2003, 157) often make students uneasy when they point out the disturbing historical relationship between Christian doctrine and the resulting assault on American Indian culture.

The issue of Native rights becomes very sensitive when we ... see how the U.S. system was built upon a 'doctrine of discovery' where *non-Christian savages and infidels* have diminished rights to their aboriginal land and, therefore, were forced (by conquest or purchase) to surrender their lands to Christians. ... Originally bestowed by the Pope and later delegated to European sovereigns, these Christian entitlements elicit a wide spectrum of student opinions and questions in our classes. The contradictions and complexities associated with issues of prosperity, honor, religion, and equity are very challenging for students who themselves struggle with questions of religion and justice.

97. Challenge naiveté.

Romanticizing or mythologizing those who are different can also limit possibilities. For example, seeing all disabled people as "amazing" or "courageous" can make it difficult to see their needs to participate in the full range of human activity, to love, laugh, and cry like everyone else.

Examine your own materials and teaching about diversity for places where balance is lacking, where information may be skewed in one direction, where arguments are neglected or weak.

In her course on disabilities, Kreston (2003, 180) stresses the fact that "Perceiving individuals as 'admirable' for simply living their lives can be as damaging as seeing them as poor, unfortunate cripples."

98. Reduce academic distance.

Authority, age, expertise, and podiums can create hierarchies and barriers that limit our connections with students. Think about ways to *increase* proximity to students. Create exercises in class where students have to consult with each other, allowing you to move around the room listening, commenting, clarifying, questioning, etc.

Bubar and Vernon (2003, 160) reference their own experiences as students to redefine what effective instruction could mean:

We try to overturn what we term 'academic distance," which defines an environment where students view teachers as privileged. This can happen when teachers do not value students, and where the teaching process is seen as a 'one-way street.' In this environment, students can simply lose confidence. ... In contrast to academic distance, we try to develop a supportive relationship with students (one that encourages honest and open dialogue), an open-door policy, and one-on-one student visits. We think these approaches send the message that students are valued, important and heard.

99. Teach resistance.

Understanding the struggles of minorities in the United States can lead to insights about the shadow side of the dominant culture, how to navigate the powerful forces of mainstream schooling and popular media and keep some sense of cultural identity alive.

Adopt the position of a marginalized group in your discipline and push for a deeper understanding of their resistance to the dominant culture. Analyze the values, attitudes, knowledge, and skills that underlie that resistance. Which would be valuable for others to emulate?

Bubar and Vernon (2003, 164-165) use the history of indigenous peoples to deconstruct dominant teachings and celebrate resistance.

For us, the most difficult aspect of teaching this class is our being able to discuss topics that directly confront the continuing colonial domination of tribal people and the institutionalization of cultural racism found within the judicial, congressional, and executive branches of our government. ... In many ways, this class teaches a form of Native resistance in an academic milieu. It allows all students to challenge the way things are.

Support Positive Change

Prejudice, bias, and oppression often spark resistance and struggle. The "fight or flight" response is hard-wired in humans as in all animals. Yet, one feature that distinguishes humans is our exceptional ability to learn and adapt. Accordingly, a pedagogy of human diversity asks that instructors devote some time and attention to balance the various human struggles for acceptance and equity with an exploration of the possibilities for positive change.

100. Think of transformation.

As important as the notion of *tolerance* is for discussions about differences and acceptance, even more is possible and desirable. A serious study of the meaning of diversity for any discipline can challenge prevailing assumptions, bring new voices into the discussion, and reorient the ways in which the world is perceived.

Look for places in your courses where a focus on diversity could actually transform what you do, what is emphasized, what is questioned, and even how students learn. You may cover less territory, but students might actually learn more, acquiring a deeper and more profound understanding of critical issues in your field.

A pedagogy of human diversity ... is 'transformative' rather than merely 'additive.' It does not simply 'add' women (or people of color) to the traditional curriculum. It changes the basic terms of the discourse; it can reset foreground and background and it recalculates norms. It requires that *all* students re-assess their places on the social map, not only those whose traditions and experiences have been ignored or misrepresented. (Canetto, Timpson, Borrayo, and Yang 2003, 277)

101. Teach activism.

Bring examples into class of what previous students have done as activists to challenge prevailing policies and practices. Share your own values, beliefs, and experiences about advocating for fairness and social justice.

In the face of widespread attacks on the supposed agendas of college professors, some instructors may shrink from making public statements about the tenets of a civilized society. Bubar and Vernon (2003, 165) argue for academic integrity here. "To some, this can look like a 'political agenda.' To us, it is about democratic ideas and basic principles of fairness. We do understand that our teaching of empowerment can lead some students to be activists for social justice, and we certainly hope it does."

102. Assign change projects.

Attempting to make changes has a way of clarifying values, galvanizing commitments, and sparking initiative. Often the biggest benefit for students is the learning that occurs once they stretch to apply classroom lessons to the world outside.

Consider replacing a more traditional academic paper or project with one that focuses on some aspect of campus change, however modest, where your students can develop greater understanding through a kind of action learning. They should identify a problem, review the available published literature, conduct interviews or surveys, develop some campus activity, analyze the results, and offer further recommendations.

As an elected state representative from northern Colorado, former university instructor Paccione (2003, 152) understands the importance of putting citizenship to work in a democracy. She writes about teaching a graduate course, "Multicultural and Special Populations," in rural Colorado:

> I don't know whether knowledge without action produces much change. ... Some students chose to focus their final investigative project on issues around education of Hispanic/Mexican students in their schools. I believe those students will help promote educational equity. ... Other students focused on redesigning the curriculum to be more culturally relevant. Although the structures of power may not be directly affected in

rural Colorado, important changes may take place in the schools.

103. Emphasize awareness and involvement.

Complex and difficult issues demand a certain degree of maturity to understand, assess, and handle emotionally. Awareness, however, is often the first step toward learning and change.

Experiment with assignments that go beyond covering content to promote a greater awareness of underlying diversity issues.

Here's an example from Bubar and Vernon (2003, 157), who describe how they help students face racism with integrity and courage.

> The subject matter found in a federal Indian law and policy class provides us with a wealth of information to challenge, engage, and teach students about cross-cultural boundaries and the fairness of our laws and treatment of North America's first inhabitants. It is through this study of history, religion, and culture that students learn to broaden their understanding. They learn to think more critically and ethically about the difficult issues. We think they become more aware and involved in the world around them.

In writing about student voices, Timpson (2003, 252) reports on the value students received from assignments that encouraged them to connect their own experiences and reactions with course readings. He quotes one student, who said, "It was a very empowering experience ... to have our experiences and beliefs drive the direction and climate of the classroom."

When you appreciate the value for your students of these kinds of assignments and accept your inherent subjectivity, you can free yourself to some extent of the usual compulsion to cover all course content and objectify student mastery of the content.

104. Choose a healthy perspective and build on hope.

The concepts we use can define our thinking. We are all, to some extent, intellectual prisoners of prevailing paradigms, the "conventional wisdom" of our age. History will eventually show how some of these concepts and paradigms were flawed or problematic.

Addressing issues of diversity may mean challenging basic assumptions today ... and even questioning the effects of our good intentions.

Here's a good example. Kreston (2003, 172-173) describes how she tries to get her students to question fundamental yet dysfunctional beliefs about disability and find new, healthy alternatives.

Many of the 'helping' professions — education, psychology, social work, occupational therapy, and human development — filter disability through a medical model perspective. ... Disability often is portrayed as personal affliction, underscoring individual differences and 'special-ness' that marginalizes rather than integrates the experience as human phenomenon. Many of the systems created for disabled people and supported by the helping professions are in direct response to this marginalization. Students who enter particular helping fields are often motivated to 'help' those less fortunate than themselves. This driving force is valued as admirable and tends to give self-worth to the person as 'helper.'

Yet, she notes,

What is often unexamined is how the pathological perspective continues to perpetuate isolation and separateness. Students who enroll in my class are required to examine their perceptions as well as question concepts they may have taken for granted. It can be quite a shock.

Addressing diversity requires a willingness to reopen old wounds and look again at the scars. What can help make this possible is a deep belief in truth and reconciliation. Here's how Bubar and Vernon (2003, 167) describe the benefits for students:

When students are empowered, when they can experience their own internal sense of mastery, their intellectual horizons can widen. They can move on with a sense of hope, a positive vision of what the future can mean for themselves and others.

Take a few minutes to explain to your students why you want to revisit old injustices, and empathize with those who struggle with the resulting feelings. Provide examples of hope where progress is being made to correct the errors of the past.

Rethink Curriculum and Expectations

A pedagogy of human diversity asks us to evaluate current course content for biases and omissions. Researching new material to counter inherited or mainstream prejudices can be very energizing for instructors and students alike.

105. Broaden the range of variation under study.

Too often, discussions about diversity are limited to questions about ethnicity, gender, sexual orientation, or religion. Thinking broadly about diversity can permit more people to join the discussion, see what is missing in the formal curriculum, and practice acceptance and appreciation.

Rethink the diversity topics you address in your courses, and consider broadening your focus. Raise the issue of diversity coverage in your department and across campus, or even ask for an institutional analysis. Look for external funds that could help jump-start a new initiative like a diversity *curriculum* infusion project funded by small grants to faculty and opportunities for professional development.

Disciplines like sociology and psychology bubble with issues of ethnicity, gender, minority status, power, identity, and the like. In disciplines like engineering and chemistry, however, it can mean a stretch for instructors to look beyond typical content coverage to find relevant and useful diversity issues.

Mona Schatz (2003, 126-127) notes that other members of the university community often say their fields have little information on cultural diversity. "Yet, I also am aware of how often we minimize cultural experiences, particularly in schools and colleges. I'm convinced that faculty and researchers in every discipline must be willing to examine their specific areas in search of diversity issues."

An enduring debate is whether diversity content should be "covered" in one course alone or infused throughout the curriculum. Perhaps the best approach would be to do both and get the benefits of both!

William Timpson (2003, 13) notes the advantages of infusing diverse content across disciplines and throughout the curriculum, contending that "diversity content is inherently interdisciplinary." Accepting this challenge can make for stimulating, important discussions about individual courses as well as entire programs. The resulting conversations can help to bridge the inherently hierarchical disciplinary silos of higher education and allow faculty to break out of their isolation as instructors. Departmental, college, and university meetings can put teaching diversity on their agendas. Resources can be identified, individual and group initiatives can be recognized, and funds can be allocated. Some success with diversity can also help build organizational capacities for taking on other issues, such as creative, nonviolent conflict resolution, peace studies, technology and teaching, instructional effectiveness, and innovation generally.

106. Address current diversity issues.

Make a commitment to stay abreast of diversity issues in your discipline, on your campus, in your community, and beyond. Keeping current is becoming easier, as news media expand and the World Wide Web grows. Connect what's in the news about diversity with scheduled topics in your classes. If you want your students to be aware of what's happening in the world, set an example for them by keeping aware and interested and by bringing the world into your classroom.

107. Teach against the grain.

Addressing neglected areas in the curriculum can invigorate your teaching and open students to new insights. Brainstorm topics in your courses that could be invigorated by "teaching against the grain" — in contradiction with conventional approaches.

Roe Bubar and Irene Vernon (2003, 153) describe how they challenge omissions and distortions in traditional college curricula and "teach against the grain":

> Our course contradicts (and adds to) the traditional approaches to the study of law and Native American peoples. Mainstream law and policy courses rarely address issues facing

tribal peoples, and few include any discussion of Indian/White relations or the richness of American Indian law and policies.

Take a zero-based approach to your course. Imagine starting your course from scratch ... and from another perspective. How would you teach about diversity?

108. Search for new material.

Anything taught over and over again runs the risk of becoming stale — even if you empower your students to take greater responsibility for learning through your course. You can keep your content fresh by experimenting with new readings, different approaches, guest speakers, etc.

Timpson (2003, 250) has gotten positive feedback from students for going beyond mainstream textbook materials: "Most of the students appreciated exposure to the real *history* of various populations and not the superficial overview that too often passes for social studies in schools. As a result, many became angry when they learned what omissions and misconceptions existed in their school texts."

There's a bonus for you, as well: as philosopher Jane Kneller (2003, 223-224) writes, finding new stories about those left out of the history of every discipline can energize instruction and learning.

109. Supplement class readings.

It is impossible to know what every student will need from us or from a particular class. We cannot possibly anticipate, considering the diversity in backgrounds, preparation, interests, motivation, and abilities.

New readings can energize your courses — and the search can energize you. Newer editions or different texts might address more salient diversity issues. The language and emphasis that different authors choose can make some texts more valuable references for the kinds of exacting analyses that deepen understanding and sharpen critical thinking.

Notice how Suzanne Tochterman (2003, 141) responds to one student's issue and makes adjustments in her class:

A student ... approached me after class and told me his religious faith led him to decide that he should not read a passage about homosexuality that I had assigned. He explained his belief that in life, one must wear 'filters' to guard from that which one finds unhealthy for one's spirit. I began to search for a course of action that could accommodate both this student and my goals for the class. I supplemented the normal class readings with additional texts that exemplified inclusiveness.

110. Use film clips for shared experiences.

Timpson (2003, 256) reports how the "use of film clips added a shared reference to course concepts and theories." One student commented, "The use of videos ... helped personalize our theories to experiences we could visualize."

Explore ways in which films and documentaries can bring important stories about diversity into your classes and provide common ground for useful discussions.

111. Use case studies.

Case studies can be presented as stories. When they are presented in narrative form, students often find them more "listenable" than lectures. Such case studies often evoke reactions in students that lead to open and active discussions. Research what case studies may already exist in your area. You can also develop your own or ask students to draw on their experiences to develop cases.

112. Teach about rights.

List the rights that people discuss in your fields. Assign students to debate the various sides of the issues that emerge.

As a follow-on to lessons on the Civil Rights movement in the 1960s, for example, a discussion of human rights generally can help students make connections to important historical events. As Bubar and Vernon (2003, 165) describe their own teaching of Federal Law and Policy,

What we teach is the recognition of rights and how they are important to any group's cultural, physical, and spiritual health. Although we focus on tribal rights, we believe that understanding rights in general and the importance of rights in the lives of all people are fundamental to maintaining them.

113. Be alert to challenges and opportunities on gender issues.

While every difference has its own specific challenges, gender relationships impact most of us directly in our personal lives. "Some have argued that an analysis of gender issues is perhaps the most difficult one to tackle because for *everybody*, gender touches upon personal relationships." (Canetto, Timpson, Borrayo, and Yang 2003, 278) Accordingly, opportunities abound in every classroom for identifying, developing, and practicing skills for effectively communication, particularly between men and women.

Identify the gender issues in your field. Select a number of provocative readings for discussion. Invite in guest speakers who can address these issues.

114. Focus on first-year seminars and orientation programs.

When first-year seminars are introduced and led well, the attention can have a positive ripple effect throughout a curriculum, sparking useful conversations about student learning among instructors all too often preoccupied with their research and specialized graduate courses.

Compose a formal letter or send an e-mail to those responsible for orientation or first-year seminars on your campus, to express your hopes for greater attention to diversity. Orientation courses can help students acquire the knowledge and develop the skills necessary to learn from diversity content and from others who are different from them.

115. Identify underlying issues.

Pay attention to any factors that may be lurking underneath your policies and practices that you have accepted without question. Evaluate your own training for biases and gaps. Use readings, interviews, and classroom observations to address areas in which you need to develop.

116. Maintain high expectations of your students.

Review previous summaries of course evaluations by your students about the degree of challenge in your classes. Students benefit most when you set standards and have expectations of them. Talk with colleagues, both within your department and across campus, about their expectations for courses at the same level as yours.

Support Personal and Professional Development

Hired as experts in their discipline areas and rewarded on many campuses for their contributions to research, college and university instructors are often pressed for time to improve their teaching and explore innovations for their courses. Whoever wants to know more about student learning or motivation quickly faces a very large body of published work. Meanwhile, advances in technology offer ever increasing possibilities that are often time-consuming to explore. To teach about human diversity and do it well may require additional study, training, and experimentation. Consequently, it becomes vital to understand the importance of personal and professional development.

117. Challenge yourself.

Teaching about diversity requires us to reflect on our own limitations, biases, and prejudices, to unlearn what is problematic and adopt new attitudes. Identify situations in your own past when you were in the minority, and list the ways in which these experiences helped you reexamine your own values, attitudes, and behaviors. Seek out situations in which you can experience being in a minority.

118. Commit to personal growth.

When we ask students to confront their own prejudices and join with others in opening up to new ideas, we would be hypocritical if we were not willing to do likewise, to reflect on our own biases and think about what more we need to learn.

List the most important professional growth experiences you have had. Now list areas in which you need to grow to better address issues of human diversity. Compare the two lists and sketch out some possible activities for yourself.

Canetto, Timpson, Borrayo, and Yang (2003, 287) come to the following conclusion:

> We ... have become convinced of the need to commit to our own personal growth as we simultaneously challenge our students to reflect, explore, rethink, and grow personally. ... As instructors, we must assume responsibility for our own personal development — for confronting our own biases as human beings while we simultaneously play the role of disciplinary experts.

Deidre Magee, a senior research assistant in the School of Education at the University of Colorado at Denver and an experienced teacher of diverse populations at many levels, told the authors of this book that: instructors *must know themselves*. She said, "When teaching diverse student populations, examining your own personal beliefs about ethnicity can help eliminate your own cultural biases." She also noted, "Teachers sometimes choose to see all students as 'just students' regardless of cultural, racial, or ethnic differences. The tendency toward a color blind view of students implies an equality that does not exist." She cited Gloria Ladson-Billings, who makes a strong argument in *The Dreamkeepers: Successful Teachers of African American Children* (33):

> Given the significance of race and color in American society, it is impossible to believe that a classroom teacher does not notice the race and ethnicity of the children she is teaching. Further, by claiming not to notice, the teacher is saying that she is dismissing one of the most salient features of the child's identity and that she does not account for it in her curricular planning and instruction. Saying we are aware of students' race and ethnic background is not the same as saying we treat students inequitably. The passion for equality in the American ethos has many teachers (and others) equating equality with sameness. . ... The notion of equity as sameness only makes sense when all students are exactly the same. ... If teachers pretend not to see students' racial and ethnic differences, they really do not see the students at all and are limited in their ability to meet their educational needs.

119. Find time to read.

The time we have as instructors seems to shrink as a direct and inverse function of the growth of knowledge in every discipline, the ever-expanding expectations on faculty for research, and the rapid spread of technology. However, we must regularly sample from the growing literature on postsecondary teaching, learning, and professional development, especially since teaching human diversity entails so many inherent challenges and complexities.

Make a commitment to identify relevant readings about teaching diversity. Share them with colleagues. Look for ways to experiment with them in your classes.

As Canetto, Timpson, Borrayo, and Yang (2003, 286) conclude, "While we often repeat the faculty mantra of 'busyness' in our efforts to stay current in our own disciplinary work, we also need to recognize the importance of systematic exposure to the education literature. Good teaching, particularly good teaching of diversity-content classes, requires studied practice and feedback. It requires that we find good readings."

120. Share strategies with colleagues.

The hectic pace of many instructor's lives often makes collaboration difficult. But the complex and sensitive issues surrounding the teaching of diversity should compel us to discuss what works, what others are facing, and what creative alternatives might be possible.

You can probably identify with the frustration and the hope expressed by Tochterman (2003, 140):

Teaching can be very isolating. ... Academics tend to retreat to the confines of their own offices. ... [They] are not used to openly discussing the art and craft of their own teaching. Although I make every effort I can to initiate dialogue with my colleagues, I find that few share what it is they do in the classroom. Instead, people will tend to talk primarily about policies and procedures. Often, when I share my strategies, I will notice that some seem to see this as threatening. I believe that if we can get others in the department to know us and our work— if we truly have a network of peers — we will feel far more empowered to act individually as well.

Meet informally with colleagues to exchange experiences and ideas. Recommend to colleagues that time be reserved at each departmental meeting for presentations on what works and discussions about what does not.

121. Understand the dynamics of peer support.

We generally recognize the benefits of cooperative learning to help students bridge differences, enhance communication, develop teamwork, and unlearn prejudices. Unfortunately, instructors get few opportunities to benefit from cooperative learning, to work with each other on classroom teaching.

Find opportunities to work with your colleagues. Form diversity teaching support groups. Develop a position paper that advocates for collegial support of teaching. Circulate it for comments and support. Submit the final version to campus leaders as well as the faculty senate or council.

122. Make use of professional growth opportunities.

It makes sense that the teaching of diversity would be improved by the use of diverse approaches to professional development, such as action learning, peer coaching, mentoring, and videotape analysis. Analyze the various mechanisms for professional development that have been used on your campus. With a few colleagues who share your commitment to diversity issues, develop a set of recommendations for campus leaders to consider. Explore the possibility of external funding. Many foundations and federal grant programs specifically target diversity.

123. Emphasize honest self-reflection.

List the various ways that your background gives you certain unique insights about particular diversity issues. Also, consider ways to broaden and deepen your experiences to better understand and appreciate the issues in teaching diversity.

124. Overcome silence.

Sometimes, for various reasons, we do not do all that we could to promote diversity. We may feel that teaching should be confined to the classroom; we may be anxious about standing out by our actions; we may have suffered for taking unpopular positions.

A good example is Mona Schatz (2003, 122-123), who describes how she reacted to the trauma of being stalked and threatened after bringing a holocaust speaker to her campus, an experience that caused her to find a position elsewhere.

> I have come to realize that this experience pushed me into a period of silence about it. When I took my new position at Colorado State University, I decided I would not talk about this experience to anyone. My fear overtly played out as anxiety and spilled into my teaching. ... Trauma survivors often use silence as a coping mechanism. ... I chose not to teach in areas that might have been construed as politically left of center. ... I stayed in 'middle-of-the-road' territory, even when addressing issues of prejudice and oppression.

Remember these words of Martin Luther King, Jr., in his "Letter from Birmingham Jail" (April 16, 1963): "We will have to repent in this generation not merely for the hateful words and actions of the bad people but for the appalling silence of the good people." In what ways would we "good people" be considered guilty of "appalling silence"? Look into your own areas of silence about issues that touch on diversity. How can you overcome your silence?

125. Develop your own communication skills.

Assess your communication skills, particularly your ability to listen deeply, to respond empathetically, and to address conflicts in class. How can you further develop those skills?

Canetto, Timpson, Borrayo, and Yang (2003, 286) note, "One form of practical professional development that may particularly benefit teachers of diversity-content classes is training in communication skills. Addressing the varied aspects of diversity — both the challenges in the content itself as well as the complexities inherent in dynamic interactions and deeper learning — instructors need to be able to listen deeply themselves, respond empathetically, identify and address conflicts that arise, and more."

126. Question your own status.

Just as we ask students to reflect deeply about their beliefs, attitudes, and values toward those who are different, we should also ask the same of ourselves. What experiences and lessons have formed our values, beliefs, and actions? Are we aware of our own privileges, status, and power as instructors?

Critically assess your role with students. Identify experiences that have made you re-evaluate your status (authority, power, control).

127. Walk your talk.

A strong argument can be made for involving students in perspective-taking activities to help them better understand and appreciate the lives and experiences of others. Instructors of diversity are likely to reap the same benefits if they too "walk their talk" and engage in activities where, for example, they become the minority person among others who are physically, behaviorally, or ideologically different.

Identify situations where you would likely hear opinions and values expressed that are very different from your own. Assess how well you are able to listen, accept, and empathize. List the insights you get for helping your students listen, accept, and empathize.

Val Middleton (2003, 105) explains how she wanted to force herself out of her comfort zone in order to gain a conscious awareness of her own values, beliefs, ethnocentricity, and privilege. "In an effort to 'walk my talk,' I wanted the experience of silently listening to someone else share values and beliefs that could likely be in opposition to mine. After thoughtful consideration, I decided to go to church after years of avoidance."

128. Support campus-wide professional development.

In any decentralized academic environment, institutional change often comes slowly. A serious commitment to promoting diversity requires more than scheduling celebrations and hosting speakers. Importantly, there is a rich literature on professional development that can provide useful ideas and guidelines.

Canetto, Timpson, Borrayo, and Yang (2003, 285) state, "We want to argue for more substantive investment in professional development. ... A campus-wide commitment to change can help overcome the inherent isolation of teachers and support their sharing, learning, growth, and creative synergy."

Identify what support would be needed to create a deeper commitment to diversity on your campus. Share your analyses with campus leaders and get their reactions.

129. Lobby for new funds for teaching diversity efforts.

When instructors develop some real skills for handling the complex, sensitive, and challenging dynamics inherent when teaching about human diversity, they become more effective at teaching in general, which justifies investing in diversity efforts.

Complete an inventory of new programs on your own campus that have received funds in the recent past. Identify what it would require to secure new funding for a teaching diversity initiative.

As new programs or initiatives are launched on campus, encourage colleagues and students to lobby for diversity components.

Deepen Your Institution's Commitment to Diversity

A pedagogy of human diversity will flourish where there is a deep institutional commitment, going beyond a traditional scheduling of ethnic celebrations and speakers. There is much important work to do above the classroom level: securing the commitment of campus leaders, recruiting supportive new hires, and infusing diversity goals within the institution's strategic planning process. Diversity is a very socially acceptable and embraceable concept in the U.S., especially for institutions of higher education: nearly all colleges and universities proclaim their support of diversity and affirm efforts to diversify their student bodies, faculty, and staff. However, institutions vary in the degree to which they are willing to go beyond the mere rhetoric of diversity. Institutions with a deep commitment to diversity provide a context in which instructors, staff, administrators, and students are aided in their work for greater understanding, acceptance, and appreciation of people who are different.

130. Recruit supportive leaders.

Only so much can be done at the classroom or instructor level. For real progress, both line and staff administrators must step forward to provide support, resources, and validation to extend this learning across the institution.

Evaluate how visionary and vigorous your campus leaders have been and on what issues. List those who can provide true leadership for a diversity-teaching initiative.

131. Use strategic planning.

Finding allies and support mechanisms is essential to making lasting progress in teaching diversity. Because every campus has some kind of formal planning process, opportunities usually exist to push institutions to perpetuate diversity initiatives.

As Canetto, Timpson, Borrayo, and Yang (2003, 288) argue, "One way to move forward is to tie this work into ongoing strategic planning. ... While any centralized planning effort has its shadow side, it also can be an important opportunity for focusing discussion and resources on important areas for change efforts."

Analyze your own institution's planning process. Identify ways to get more formal attention for teaching diversity.

132. Create action plans.

Institutional diversity goals must be translated into action plans. Simply having a document that serves public relations does not guarantee that stated goals will be reached. Push to move your campus efforts to support diversity from rhetoric into action. Identify initiatives that have been successful and use them as models. Plans must specify personnel, responsibilities, timelines, and resources. Also, it is vital to involve various underrepresented groups in the decision-making process.

133. Hire and retain diverse personnel.

Too often, individuals in a minority status on campus by virtue of their gender, ethnicity, sexual orientation, or physical ability are significantly underrepresented among full-time tenured faculty. Assertive recruitment and retention strategies are needed to ensure that the diversity of the population is represented at all levels within our institutions.

Create a task force or study group to investigate efforts at diversifying your faculty and staff. Prepare and distribute a position paper with concrete recommendations for needed improvements. Distribute it widely. Make appointments to discuss your ideas with campus leaders. Work with contacts in the local and state media who can help circulate your concerns and ideas to the general public.

134. Pay attention to campus artifacts as signifiers.

"Campus artifacts (artwork, signs, posters, and architectural features) can signify four different approaches to or levels of institutional commitment (Banning, Deniston, and Middleton, 2000) in regard to how diversity is being promoted," according to James Banning (2003, 212-213). He describes this framework:

- NEGATIVE APPROACH: Overt and subtle examples may indicate that an institution really does not support diversity. For example, racist, sexist, or homophobic graffiti that is not promptly removed from restroom walls can create a very hostile environment and undermine institutional pronouncements or programs on valuing diversity.

- NULL APPROACH: When institutional environments lack either negative or positive artifacts, the result is not neutral, but null. In other words, a "neutral" environment can be inherently discriminatory when it has been developed and maintained to reflect "white male privilege."

- CONTRIBUTIVE/ADDITIVE APPROACH: Institutions have some cultural artifacts in their environments that support diversity, but only those with which the dominant culture is comfortable.

- TRANSFORMATIONAL/SOCIAL ACTION APPROACH: Institutions can be characterized by two key factors: they send messages from a diversity-centric perspective rather than a majority-centric perspective and they call for a commitment to personal involvement and change (deep diversity).

Use the above framework to analyze what your own campus is doing to support diversity. Share this with allies. Make revisions based on the feedback you receive, solicit endorsements, and submit it to campus leaders for their reaction.

135. Advocate for "zero tolerance" policies.

Institutions with a deep level of commitment to diversity have policies in place that do not tolerate acts of discrimination, prejudice, or hate toward any group on their campuses. Moreover, "zero tolerance" policies are actively pursued with those involved in such acts.

Explore what policies are in place on your own campus. Develop recommendations for needed changes, recruit supporters, and send these to senior campus leaders for reaction and further discussion.

Here's an extreme example of what can happen.

In 1998, Matthew Shepard, a student at the University of Wyoming in Laramie was beaten to death in an act reportedly of hate toward gays and lesbians. Following this incident, a group of students at nearby Colorado State University were in a homecoming parade float that carried words and images disparaging Shepard and homosexuality in general. Immediately CSU placed these students on probation and put in place an action plan to educate these students about the dangerous implications of their prejudice and hatred.

136. Seek support from administrators and other allies.

The support of college or university administration for faculty teaching diversity is fundamental. Administrators need to recognize the array of complex issues that arise in preparing students to become "diversity competent" in whatever professions they are pursuing. Administrators demonstrate support in this context by endorsing and creating conditions in which these faculty can develop their skills without feeling anxious about negative reactions.

Faculty should also seek to involve *diversity allies* in their efforts.

In their chapter in *Resistance to Multiculturalism*, Laurie Roades and Jeffery Mio (2000) define "diversity allies" as individuals from a dominant group who not only value diversity but actively participate in helping people become more inclusive and embracing of underrepresented diverse groups. Eric Aoki (2003, 93) addresses the key role that other *allies* (mentors, colleagues, and peers) have played in encouraging him to share in class personal elements of himself that are relevant and important to the content under study.

James Banning, who teaches in the School of Education at Colorado State University, provided the authors of this book with this recommendation for getting support for teaching about human diversity when more traditional channels run dry. He says, "Go Guerrilla!"

> Guerrilla as a concept is now attached to nearly all phases of our society. ... Guerrilla action encompasses unconventional, non-sanctioned, outside the mainstream, unusual tactics to attain an objective. ... Going Guerrilla for diversity means finding ways to reach diversity objectives by strategies and tactics that are outside of traditional institutional strategies. Typical institutional strategies include appointed task forces, study groups, special committees, special funds, offices and budgets, and other officially sanctioned activities. 'Going Guerrilla' means finding strategies and tactics outside those just mentioned,

those that do not need to have institutional sanction. Here are just a few strategies:

- Form informal groups of faculty within departments and across departments to engage in mutual support of diversity goals.

- Bring faculty together to write about their experiences.

- Develop research agendas related to the many issues of campus diversity (including institutional research into related issues of recruitment, campus climate, success experiences, graduation rates, etc.).

- Help student groups form and advocate for diversity goals.

- Take an active 'editorial stance' regarding diversity issues in the campus and community news outlets.

Contribute to the Scholarship of Teaching Diversity

One very encouraging mechanism for change is work on the scholarship of teaching. We ourselves have been energized by the challenges of writing this book and *Teaching Diversity*. Without additional resources, we came together because we all felt deeply about the issues we faced. We developed new relationships as we listened to each other's stories. We shared readings and discussed their implications. We gave each other feedback on drafts of our own chapters. Through this work, we know that we have improved our own teaching. In addition, we each received credit for a publication in our annual performance reviews and for tenure and promotion decisions. We hope that others will not only benefit from our work on these books but also get ideas for energizing their own campuses to make a deeper commitment to teaching diversity well.

137. Conduct research on diversity.

The issues we face as instructors, because of our natural curiosity, will often be what we find most meaningful, interesting, and rewarding. Researching a problem can get us thinking more systematically, e.g., clarifying a problem at hand, reviewing relevant reports or studies, collecting and analyzing data from surveys, observations, interviews, student exams, and papers, thinking through the themes that emerge, and exploring various implications in our classes.

Reflect on the reactions of your students when you introduce diversity topics. Identify the range of responses that you have witnessed. How could you better understand what your students are feeling?

138. Write about your teaching.

"Raising the stakes" is a phrase that is used on stage and screen to describe how writers attempt to capture and keep the attention of the audience. When a life is at risk, for example, or a disaster looms large, we tend to engage more in the story. It gives us more reason to care about the characters. In a similar way, writing for publication can "raise the stakes" for an instructor, translating personal experiences in a way that generalizes and can benefit others.

Make a commitment to write about some aspect of your teaching to present at a conference or publish. Reflect on the impact of this writing on your own thinking and teaching.

139. Lobby for institutional support for research.

Teaching well has its challenges. On a campus where rewards are heavily skewed toward research — an unfortunate reality on too many American campuses — teaching well is even more challenging. The situation is even worse for instructors teaching diversity content, which demands even more skill and sophistication. The scholarship of teaching, however, holds much promise for focusing the talents of disciplinary experts on the challenges that students face in learning about diversity.

Identify leaders on your own campus who might support the scholarship of teaching. Make a proposal for some seed monies. To help bridge the historic division between research and teaching, submit a proposal for a book of case studies that specializes in postsecondary education, innovation, and change.

Support Diversity by Globalizing the Curriculum

In the U.S., we can become preoccupied by the "big stories" of our own populations —immigration, assimilation, slavery, feminism, Native sovereignty, sexual orientation, civil rights, religious persecution, disabilities rights, and so on. Stories from other countries and cultures, however, can provide valuable references for discussions about other possibilities, assumptions, and values. Support for a focus on human diversity is pervasive at American institutions of higher education. For many institutions this can also translate into a greater appreciation for a more global curriculum.

140. Connect to the world on campus.

Consistent with the globalization movement, one goal for teaching about human diversity is to broaden students' knowledge of the human experience and prepare them for professional, community, and family roles in an increasingly diverse and global society.

Take advantage of the presence of international students, faculty, and staff on your campus. For example, ask students to conduct interviews or focus group sessions with members of these various communities, covering issues related to the course content under study. Your students may learn that there are many other viable views about the world, views that might differ greatly from their own.

141. Help students see their world through other lenses.

One way to globalize the curriculum is to ask students to explain themselves through the perspectives of people outside the U.S. With the explosion of the World Wide Web and satellite television, access to the perspectives of people around the world is within easy reach.

Explore using international speakers, films, news outlets, and Web sites in your classes. For example, you can create assignments that have students identify issues relevant to their own course of study and compare the coverage in media abroad with what local and/or U.S. national outlets contain. Where language barriers exist, software can provide instant translation of texts. Encourage your students to discuss the views from other countries.

142. Expand student worldviews.

The European-American canon that dominates the U.S. academic curriculum in the social sciences and humanities tends to confirm our students' worldviews; courses on diversity often challenge them. Exposing your students to global perspectives can help them think "outside of the box" generally. Include readings from international journals or books in your courses that can provide alternate views on particular topics.

143. Put students on a social map.

Teaching about human diversity engages students with issues of equity, justice, power, and powerlessness. It exposes students to the social influences in people's lives and to the consequences of these influences in terms of status and opportunities.

Re-evaluate tensions and conflicts that have surfaced in previous classes when topics of human diversity arise. Reframe these as potential opportunities or catalysts for deeper understanding and intellectual and emotional growth.

We should challenge our students to think about their privileges and oppression and about their place on the social map, particularly in a global context. Learning about social stratification and inequalities can be threatening because it challenges how our students perceive their place in the world.

However, it is important to realize that these negative reactions are not necessarily problematic. Rather, they are normal when the material makes students uncomfortable. These negative reactions frustrate and even exhaust us as instructors, but we should not avoid risking them, as they offer our students opportunities for cognitive and emotional learning. The intense dynamics of diversity-content classes can also stimulate us to grow as teachers, but only if we take them as occasions to better understand how to help our students come to terms with their issues of social identity and social status.

144. Recognize the validity of other worldviews.

Invite students who have had the opportunity to travel, study, or live abroad to open a discussion about the acceptance of other worldviews.

James Boyd (2003) encourages students to see other cultures as being as valid as their own. This can help them draw on their own experiences to better understand the existential and conceptual coherence of diverse worldviews and religions. It is almost automatic for Western students to think of other religions as merely different approaches to the same truth (what Carl Jung calls the "monotheism of consciousness"). Helping students recognize valid differences becomes easier when students have lived in other countries and radically different cultures, which emphasizes the importance of study abroad programs and other cross-cultural experiences for our students.

145. Understand the world with story and metaphor.

Share stories from your own experiences with other cultures. Explore their value in opening up a more personal, honest, and revealing conversation about differences, acceptance, empathy, and learning.

Boyd (2003, 65) suggests that telling about his own personal experiences abroad — his study of religion, his struggles and breakthroughs, overcoming his attitudes, beliefs, and emotions — helps students think about their journeys through his courses in new, memorable, and powerful ways. "My experience has been that if I can harness the emotional and intellectual energy they bring to this subject, positive or negative, I may have a chance to teach them something significant enough to touch their lives in an enriching way."

146. Meet the world through music.

Try using music from different cultures and subcultures to start and/or end a particular class. You can also play music when students complete a free-write. Invite students to share some of their favorite music that connects with different diversity topics.

Boyd (2003, 72) starts and ends each class period with the musical sounds of a particular culture — "admittedly a poor imitation of being immersed in another culture." Although we may think of music as a universal language, like language it differs across cultures: the meanings of music depend greatly on explicit and implicit cultural associations.

147. Approach the world with empathy.

When we approach the world with empathy, we show understanding and sensitivity to the feelings, thoughts, and experience of others. This is different from objectivity, the neutrality usually expected in academic study. Discuss the twin challenges of simultaneous holding on to "empathy" and "neutrality" when thinking about those who are different. Recognize that the resulting tensions can be powerful catalysts for intellectual and emotional development.

Epilogue: Lessons Learned

William Timpson

As a postscript to *147 Practical Tips for Teaching Diversity*, we asked contributors to reflect on their experiences in working on this project and respond to a written survey about any changes to their own thinking. From the very beginning, we hoped that our own experiences in working on this project, individually and collectively, could provide some useful insights.

Terry Deniston has been actively involved in teaching diversity for many years. We recruited her to bring a fresh perspective to this epilogue.

Entering the Great Conversation
Terry Deniston

It was more than ten years ago when I sat with rapt attention listening to Rexford Brown speak at an Inclusion Conference in Denver, Colorado, telling his story about traveling to a school on a reservation. One particularly poignant moment was when he read aloud from his 1991 book the story of a medicine man who admonished his people for "losing touch with what he believed was a higher literacy: an inheritance of stories and legends that give meaning to ordinary language and daily life" (Brown 1991, 90-91). In the conclusion of this reservation school case study, Rex wrote that educators on this reservation were trying to

> guide [their students] through the broadening of their circles, the intersections of their circles with other people's circles, people old and young, modern and ancient. Let them weave themselves into the tapestry of their culture, and show them now and then that they have done so. Make them reflect sometimes on how what they have said and written matches or con-

flicts with what others have said and written, in their own culture and in others. Show them that, all on their own, they have entered into a great conversation.

As I listened, I was sorry that I was not in the "great conversation" of which he spoke, but I wanted to be. I wanted to be a part of the original event. I had much the same reaction in late September 2004, when I watched many of the authors whose tips are in this text tell their stories. As a part of our University's Diversity Summit, many of these authors were sharing their tips and experiences about teaching diversity at the university level. Again, I felt a little cheated and left out of the main event, which had been the project of writing this book. These authors/discussants had come to know each other's work very well through this writing project and at the Diversity Summit they would remind each other to tell about this story or that event, this way of setting clear expectations or that way of norming the group. They commented with surprise when one author sat instead of stood to speak and offered or noted other nuances or inside information that let the audience know that they had become their own community. And, it was Bill [Timpson] who, like the medicine man, was connecting their stories together and facilitating this great conversation.

I wonder if that is how you are feeling having come to the end of this text. Well, let me reassure you that if you are reading this book you are, like me, a member of a much larger conversation. You may attend diversity and inclusion workshops. You may read other books like this one. In the final analysis, you treasure the opportunities to converse with other people who "get it," and you try to live out values that affirm diversity in your personal and professional life. I wonder, too, if you long for the community that was lived in this text, an association with others who reflect on their own practice and generously share their tips with others along the way.

I was invited to contribute these comments by Bill Timpson and Jim Banning, who hold a vision about what universities and schools should be about in their classrooms and across departments. As I thought about this work in the context of my own professional life, it was inspiring for me to consider that as policy makers in our state started calling diversity the "D" word and were enacting new standards for teacher licensure that forbade the use of the word, Bill began calling his "tribe" together to collaborate on *Teaching Diversity*. As some university students and legislators in our state began to advocate for a Student Bill of Rights so that "students would feel protected from liberal professors on campus," Bill and the other editors once again gathered colleagues together to create this text, *147 Practical Tips for Teaching Diversity*. I know that these events were not completely linear nor necessarily connected events, but to me, as a teacher of teachers, it feels particularly synchronous, because these texts serve as acts of resilience and hope in an oppressive political climate.

James Banks, a scholar who is often considered one of the originators and most influential leaders in this attention to teaching diversity, was asked for his closing comments on multicultural education in an interview with *NEA Today*. He responded, "I think we need to know, to care, and to act, because I think in that way we can help transform ourselves and help transform the world" (1998, 12). At Colorado State University, we have these books as a manifestation of this transformation. We have learned more about ourselves and others by becoming a collaborative writing community of teachers and scholars who spent hours reflecting on our own practices, reacting to the ideas of others, and, finally, creating these "tips" to share with you. We hope our work inspires you to join us and others in this great conversation.

> The academy is not paradise. But learning is a place where paradise can be created. The classroom, with all its limitations, remains a location of possibility. In that field of possibility we have the opportunity to labor for freedom, to demand of ourselves and our comrades, an openness of mind and heart that allows us to face reality even as we collectively imagine ways to move beyond boundaries, to transgress. This is education as the practice of freedom. (hooks 1994, 207)

✹✹✹

Jim Banning, researcher, teacher, and contributor to this text and wonders about a lot of things, asked the book's contributors to write about their work and how it impacted their thinking about the curriculum, their choice of texts and readings, their teaching, and their interactions with students. Shelby Maier is a doctoral student in Human Development and Family Studies who conducted an analysis of the themes or "tips" that emerged from the *Teaching Diversity* text itself. Below are what these teachers and authors identified from this collaborative effort and that of *Teaching Diversity*. Using content analysis, Banning and Maier identified the themes in the following section.

Lessons Learned
Jim Banning and Shelby Maier

THEME 1: INDIVIDUAL STORIES

If we believe, as the medicine man advised, that we must understand our own stories first, it will be helpful to understand the individual authors' experiences of writing in this text.

> "Having others share and present their writing kept me focused and on task to write myself."

> "[This was an] energizing project. I enjoyed co-writing the chapter .... It made me focus on aspects of my teaching and the philosophical approach I was actually using."

> "In writing for Teaching Diversity, I learned the following: making oneself vulnerable and exposing one's life's challenges and cultural struggles ... liberates some and makes others uncomfortable."

> "The ways in which we write as academics can be diverse if we support them as such. Research is inevitably connected to the self and the ways in which we train ourselves to see the world."

> "I became more aware of the 'depth of experience' in diversity of my colleagues. ...Their personal stories gave new understanding of not only diversity, but a new understanding of my colleagues."

> "Most of what we talk and write about has much to do with the content areas in the humanities and social and behavioral sciences. We have little to do with the 'bench sciences' and related areas. I'm not sure why this is."

> "The first thing [I thought about] was how diverse peoples' reactions are to issues of diversity in the classroom. To say that instructors' and students' reactions were multifaceted seems like an understatement. [Reactions] were inevitably both emotional and cognitive/intellectual. I realize that this sounds presumptuous, but is wasn't clear to me as I read some of the chapters that even the authors recognized how diverse their responses were, because their recommendations appeared to lack coherence."

> "Various contributors attended one or more meetings over three years, read [some of] each other's chapter drafts, as well as, other articles and chapters sent around. Each contributor responded to writ-

ten feedback from one or more of the editors. While contributors knew they would get a publication, the conversations were also inherently compelling: a terrific professional development activity on a topic of great interest to the campus, national audiences and ourselves."

"The editors' tireless efforts to get people together, collaborate, and promote the work for this book was above and beyond."

"It did make me think more about confidentiality and its limits within a classroom environment. Are our classroom teaching experiences ours to analyze, think about and write about? Are there limits to this? What are students' right to confidentiality, if any?"

THEME 2: IMPACT ON TEACHING

For teaching at any level, a central focus for assessment must always be on student experiences and learning. We believe that this is especially important when we teach about diversity. We also want to assert that the parallel is true for any collaboration among instructors: any final assessment must examine the impact on instructors' thinking and practice. In response to our written survey, several contributors commented on the impact on their own teaching: their choice of texts and activities, their awareness of diversity issues, and what is means to have a safe, respectful, caring, and inclusive classroom.

While many instructors routinely ask their students to stop and reflect on their own experiences in class and hear from their classmates, these authors/instructors rarely afford themselves this same opportunity.

"I was able to review my pedagogy and in-class behavior from the specific vantage point of how they reflect issues of diversity. I had only reflected on these matters in piecemeal fashion in the past."

"[This project] has made me reflect on various issues, i.e., the curriculum, my choice of texts and readings, my teaching, and my interactions with students."

"I'm choosing more provocative titles now."

"I'm more attentive to disability issues for class readings."

"I will say I benefited from [reading what others wrote], but what was really beneficial was the process [of working together on this project]."

Several contributors wrote about issues of safety when addressing diversity, both for students and themselves. One respondent to our survey returned to that theme when commenting on the need for reflection.

"[This project] made me think about what our role is in challenging students in their beliefs and prejudices while creating an accepting environment in which all opinions are allowed a voice."

Several contributors also remarked on their increased sensitivity to the needs of diverse populations generally.

"I have more ideas for infusing diversity into my various courses."

"I seek more sharing of in-depth personal stories from the students."

"While it may be unrealistic to address the full range of diversity topics, it is important to include mention of as many diverse identities as possible, to invite a broad and inclusive spectrum for how we define diversity."

"I see interconnections among the various possibilities for considering diversity and how better to reach majority students, in particular."

A number of respondents remarked on their increased sensitivity to the needs of specific populations.

DISABILITIES: "I was acutely reminded that after reading Rosemary Kreston's [2003] chapter that I have been insufficiently sensitive to this perspective. I use more examples from friends and family who have shared their struggles and lessons of various disabilities."

RELIGION: "I've been more thoughtful regarding religion in multiple modes of the spiritual, philosophical, moral, political and cultural."

SOCIAL CLASS: "More time spent thinking and talking about the interaction between education and social class privilege."

GENDER: "I've been focusing more on problems within masculinity constructions."

ETHNICITY: "I've asked my students to help me define the ethnic groups and issues they would most like to learn about in class ... for the ethnicity and communication presentation."

GEOGRAPHY: "I address regionalism in the U.S. earlier in class discussions ... and then talk about how the remaining diversity variables can be differently addressed depending on region."

INTERNATIONAL: "[I have become more attentive to the needs of students from outside the U.S.] through my conversations with Silvia and Evelinn and reading their chapter."

THEME 3: NAMING SOME OF THE BARRIERS

The opportunity to reflect on this collaborative project raised other related issues and questions. For example, we see the potential benefits of discussions between and among instructors who are otherwise isolated by the nature of the work and their own disciplinary sub-specializations. We think that any college or university could gain much by utilizing the various "tips" identified here as catalysts for campus-wide discussions about its own institutional goals.

"The lack of wider interest on campus reinforces the perception that teaching is truly undervalued at a research university."

"The scholarship of teaching can effectively bridge the domains of research and teaching."

"It's disappointing that there is not more interest across campus in an original work of scholarship in an area of supposedly high interest and commitment."

"[We should be working] for more explicit intersection of diversity variables across the board."

"A discomforting thing is that most of us (contributing to this project) are political liberals. ... There is some research that shows that bench science faculty tend toward political conservatism. What if our book is really, in its broader sense, about one aspect of political liberalism in the university and the reason no one from Engineering, for example, wrote a chapter was because we subtly excluded them?"

THEME 4: FUTURE DIRECTIONS

Clearly, this experience has whetted the writers' appetites for future endeavors. Instead of concerns about the time required, what emerged were ideas for more and different conversations and activities, including how best to interface with the larger university community.

"Spend more time with colleagues and their stories."

"Include several published chapters of interviews/conversations between two scholars reflecting on cultural issues from diverse/different identity positionalities."

"Secure university support, resources, leadership, etc., if possible, so as to capture the synergy of faculty and staff on campus working on a topic of significant importance to the university."

"Other collaborative projects would be possible with some university support."

✳✳✳

Final Thoughts
William Timpson

In many ways, the writing of these two books — *Teaching Diversity* and *147 Practical Tips for Teaching Diversity* — sparked a stimulating, complex, and ultimately productive interaction among university faculty and staff otherwise isolated from each other by the nature of their subdisciplinary expertise, the unwillingness of campus leaders to promote effective professional development, and the lack of commitment by the university generally to quality instruction. The value of professional development is often overshadowed by the isolating reality of academic work and its reward structure. Talent may go undeveloped. Spirits may sag. Possibilities for institutional synergy can be lost.

Yet, strikingly, these same barriers make the work and the scholarship of teaching especially beneficial, for it can be through research on instruction that discussion of promising classroom practices is elevated to a more rigorous, research-based level, and contributors can be given more credit for their innovations and efforts. In a day of shrinking resources, colleges and universities can benefit much from projects such as the one undertaken to produce these two particular books of original scholarship. The kind of process modeled here can attract faculty from different disciplines to spend considerable time together on a topic of shared concern with minimal additional resources. The fact that the contributors to these two books spent five years in ongoing discussions seems especially remarkable, given the demands on faculty at a Carnegie Extensive research university like Colorado State University.

It is our hope that this book provides one model to move in a positive direction. We all benefited from the energetic and integrative leadership of faculty who recruited potential contributors, set an agenda and a timetable to frame the process, and facilitated regular meetings for the sharing of ideas, concerns, drafts, and feedback.

References

Allen, Katherine R. 1995. Opening the classroom closet — sexual orientation and self-disclosure. *Family Relations,* 44(2): 136-141.

Aoki, Eric. 2003. Making space in the classroom for my gay identity: A letter I've been wanting to write. In *Teaching Diversity,* edited by William M. Timpson, Silvia Sara Canetto, Evelinn A. Borrayo, and Raymond Yang. Madison, WI: Atwood Publishing.

Banks, James. 1998. Extra! Extra! Dr. James A. Banks on multicultural education. *NEA Today.* National Education Association. www.nea.org/neatoday/9809/banks.html.

Banning, James H. 2003. The institution's commitment to diversity: An aid or hindrance to teachers of diversity? In *Teaching Diversity,* edited by William M. Timpson, Silvia Sara Canetto, Evelinn A. Borrayo, and Raymond Yang. Madison, WI: Atwood Publishing.

Banning, James H., Terry Deniston, and Val Middleton. 2000. A visual anthropological taxonomy for assessing equity climate. Paper presented at the annual meeting of the National Coalition for Sex Equity. Denver, CO, July.

Belenky, Mary Field, Blythe McVicker Clinchy, Nancy Rule Goldberger, and Jill Mattuck Tarule. 1986. *Women's ways of knowing: The development of self, voice, and mind.* New York: Basic Books.

Brendtro, Larry K., Martin Brokenleg, and Steve Van Bockern. 1990. *Reclaiming youth at risk: Our hope for the future.* Bloomington, IN: National Educational Service.

Boyd, James W. 2003. Teaching the diversity of world religions. In *Teaching Diversity,* edited by William M. Timpson, Silvia Sara Canetto, Evelinn A. Borrayo, and Raymond Yang. Madison, WI: Atwood Publishing.

Brown, Rexford G. 1991. *Schools of thought: How the politics of literacy shape thinking in the classroom.* San Francisco: Jossey-Bass.

Bubar, Roe, and Irene Vernon. 2003. A native perspective on teaching law and U.S. policy: The inclusion of federal Indian law and policy in a college curriculum. In *Teaching Diversity,* edited by William M. Timpson, Silvia Sara Canetto, Evelinn A. Borrayo, and Raymond Yang. Madison, WI: Atwood Publishing.

Canetto, Silvia Sara, and Evelinn A. Borrayo. 2003. Alien perspectives in accented voices: Classroom dynamics when international female instructors teach diversity content. In *Teaching Diversity,* edited by William M. Timpson, Silvia Sara Canetto, Evelinn A. Borrayo, and Raymond Yang. Madison, WI: Atwood Publishing.

Canetto, Silvia Sara, William M. Timpson, Evelinn Borrayo, and Raymond Yang. 2003. Teaching about human diversity: Lessons learned and recommendations. In *Teaching Diversity*, edited by William M. Timpson, Silvia Sara Canetto, Evelinn A. Borrayo, and Raymond Yang. Madison, WI: Atwood Publishing.

Davies, Timothy Gray. 2003. Experiencing diversity in distance learning. In *Teaching Diversity*, edited by William M. Timpson, Silvia Sara Canetto, Evelinn A. Borrayo, and Raymond Yang. Madison, WI: Atwood Publishing.

Gardner, Howard. 1983. *Frames of mind: The theory of multiple intelligences.* New York: Basic Books.

———. 1999. *Intelligence reframed: Multiple intelligences for the twenty-first century.* New York: Basic Books.

Gilligan, Carol. 1982. *In a different voice: Psychological theory and woman's development.* Cambridge, MA: Harvard University Press.

Goleman, Daniel. 1995. *Emotional intelligence.* New York: Bantam.

hooks, bell. 1994. *Teaching to transgress: Education as the practice of freedom.* London: Routledge.

Kees, Nathalie. 2003. Creating safe learning environments. In *Teaching Diversity*, edited by William M. Timpson, Silvia Sara Canetto, Evelinn A. Borrayo, and Raymond Yang. Madison, WI: Atwood Publishing.

Kneller, Jane. 2003. Recalling the canon. In *Teaching Diversity*, edited by William M. Timpson, Silvia Sara Canetto, Evelinn A. Borrayo, and Raymond Yang. Madison, WI: Atwood Publishing.

Kreston, Rose. 2003. Disability as part of the diversity curriculum. In *Teaching Diversity*, edited by William M. Timpson, Silvia Sara Canetto, Evelinn A. Borrayo, and Raymond Yang. Madison, WI: Atwood Publishing.

Ladson-Billings, Gloria. 1994. *The dreamkeepers: Successful teachers of African American children.* San Francisco: Jossey-Bass Publishers.

Lowman, Joseph. 1995. *Mastering the techniques of teaching.* Second edition. San Francisco: Jossey-Bass.

Maslow, Abraham. 1954. *Motivation and personality.* New York: Harper and Row.

———. 1959. *New knowledge in human values.* New York: Harper and Row.

Middleton, Val. 1997. Preservice teachers: Beliefs about diversity and multicultural commitment. Unpublished doctoral dissertation. Colorado State University, Fort Collins.

——— 2003. Reaching the congregation, not just the choir: Conquering resistance to diversity issues. In *Teaching Diversity*, edited by William M. Timpson, Silvia Sara Canetto, Evelinn A. Borrayo, and Raymond Yang. Madison, WI: Atwood Publishing.

Paccione, Angela V. 2003. *E pluribus unum*: Teaching diversity in rural Colorado. In *Teaching Diversity*, edited by William M. Timpson, Silvia Sara Canetto, Evelinn A. Borrayo, and Raymond Yang. Madison, WI: Atwood Publishing.

Perry, William G. 1981. Cognitive and ethical growth: The making of meaning. In *The Modern American College: Responding to the New Realities of Diverse Students and a Changing Society,* edited by Arthur W. Chickering. San Francisco: Jossey-Bass.

———. 1999. *Forms of intellectual and ethical development in the college years: A scheme.* San Francisco: Jossey-Bass.

Roades, Laurie A., and Jeffery Scott Mio. 2000. Allies: How are they created and what are their experiences? In *Resistance to Multiculturalism: Issues and Interventions,* edited by Jeffery Scott Mio and Gene I. Awakuni Basingstoke. Hampshire, United Kingdom: Brunner-Routledge/Taylor and Francis Group.

Salovey, Peter, and John. D. Mayer. 1990. Emotional intelligence. *Imagination, Cognition, and Personality*, 9(3): 185-211.

———. 1997. *Emotional development and emotional intelligence.* New York: Basic Books.

Timpson, William M. 1999. *Metateaching and the instructional map.* (Teaching Techniques/Strategies Series, V. 1.) Madison, WI: Atwood Publishing.

———. 2003. Walking our talk: The special challenges of teaching diversity. In *Teaching Diversity*, edited by William M. Timpson, Silvia Sara Canetto, Evelinn A. Borrayo, and Raymond Yang. Madison, WI: Atwood Publishing.

Timpson, William M., Silvia Sara Canetto, Evelinn A. Borrayo, and Raymond Yang, eds. 2003. *Teaching diversity: Challenges and complexities, identities and integrity.* Madison, WI: Atwood Publishing.

Tochterman, Suzanne. 2003. Majority as minority: Transferring lessons learned from teaching k-12 inner-city students to the university. In *Teaching Diversity*, edited by William M. Timpson, Silvia Sara Canetto, Evelinn A. Borrayo, and Raymond Yang. Madison, WI: Atwood Publishing.

Yang, Raymond K. 2003. Socratic and therapeutic underpinnings of self-disclosure in the classroom. In *Teaching Diversity*, edited by William M. Timpson, Silvia Sara Canetto, Evelinn A. Borrayo, and Raymond Yang. Madison, WI: Atwood Publishing.

About the Authors

WILLIAM M. TIMPSON
Professor, School of Education, Colorado State University

SILVIA SARA CANETTO
Professor, Department of Psychology, Colorado State University

EVELINN A. BORRAYO
Assistant Professor, Department of Psychology, Colorado State University

RAYMOND YANG
Professor, Department of Psychology, Colorado State University

ERIC AOKI
Associate Professor, Department of Speech Communication, Interpersonal and Cultural Communication, Colorado State University

JAMES H. BANNING
Professor, School of Education, Colorado State University

JAMES W. BOYD
University Distinguished Teaching Scholar; Professor, Department of Philosophy, Colorado State University

ROE BUBAR
Assistant Professor, Social Work, Colorado State University

TIMOTHY GRAY DAVIES
Professor, School of Education, Colorado State University

NATHALIE KEES
    Associate Professor, Counseling and Career Development, School of Education, Colorado State University

JANE KNELLER
    Associate Professor, Department of Philosophy, Colorado State University

ROSEMARY KRESTON
    Director, Resources for Disabled Students; Instructor, The "Handicapped" Individual in Society, Colorado State University

CHANCE W. LEWIS
    Assistant Professor, School of Education, Colorado State University

VALERIE A. MIDDLETON
    Assistant Professor, Teaching and Learning, Northern Arizona State University

ANGELA PACCIONE
    School of Education, Colorado State University and Elected Representative, Colorado House District 53, 2002-2006

NINA S. ROBERTS
    Education and Outreach Specialist, National Park Service, Colorado State University

MONA C. S. SCHATZ
    Professor, School of Social Work; Director, Education and Research Institute for Fostering Families, Colorado State University

SUZANNE TOCHTERMAN
    VATS I&R Coordinator for Kellar Institute for Human Disabilities, George Mason University

IRENE S. VERNON
    Director, Center for Applied Studies in American Ethnicity (CASAE); Professor, English Department and CASAE, Colorado State University